BITE BACK BETTER

Here are 52 of the most popular
American Appetizer Recipes
with a presidential touch.

Paul Lloyd Hemphill

For permission requests, contact:
One White's Pond Press
In partnership with **American Education Defenders, Inc.**
AmericanEducationDefenders.org
paul@americaneducationdefenders.org

Grayscale Edition
BITE BACK BETTER,
Part of the **Back Better** Series – Book 2 of 3
Paperback ISBN (grayscale interior): 979-8-9926879-3-4
Library of Congress Control Number: 2025906605

Design by Imesh and interior layout by the Author
Published by One White's Pond Press

Subjects / Categories:
COOKING / Courses & Dishes / Appetizers
BIOGRAPHY & AUTOBIOGRAPHY / Presidents & Heads of State
SELF-HELP / Motivational & Inspirational

This book is a work of creative nonfiction. While the character traits, values, and presidential references are based on historical figures, commentary on presidential legacies are dramatized for educational and inspirational purposes.

To
my son Mark and his wife Charinee
whose generosity gave my wife,
Ann Marie, and me
two weeks of pure joy in Italy,
unforgettable memories,
and a lifetime of gratitude.

Also by Paul Lloyd Hemphill

BOOKS
Gettysburg Lessons In The Digital Age
Why You're Already A Leader
Inspiration For Skeptics
Max Your Leadership*!*
Laughing With Leaders
Inspiration For Teens
You're Awesome!
Hair Force One
Planning For College
How To Play The College Game
Back Better Series In 3 Books
Bake Back Better
Bite Back Better
Bond Back Better
and
Funnies of the Presidents (ChaiGPT)
Surviving Teen Chaos (ChatGPT)
Watching Paint Dry (ChatGPT)

VIDEOS
America's 52 Stories

INTRODUCTION

Bite Back Better is not your average cookbook. It's part snack attack, part history lesson, and part undercover parenting tool designed to get your kids talking—without them even realizing it. Every recipe in here comes with a true story from a U.S. president and a value like honesty, fairness, or perseverance. You'll laugh, you'll learn, and—bonus—you might even end up with something delicious.

Before You Dig In...about the pictures: many of the presidential images in this book were generated with the help of ChatGPT. So if a few of them look like your Uncle Bob in a wig or someone running for prom king instead of president... well, blame the robot. I focused on the stories and snacks—you know, where it counts.

Let's be clear: these presidential snack pairings are totally made up. Lincoln next to cheeseballs? Yeah, I went there. I have no idea what he actually ate (though I'm guessing not nachos). The history is real—the food matches are just here to keep things interesting and fun.

Why 52 recipes? Because **once a week** sounds manageable. It gives you 52 chances a year to say, "Put down your phone and help me make this," and 52 chances for your kid to say, "Wait! Andrew Jackson did *what*?!"

This book is also about **character,** and no, not the kind in video games or cartoons. I mean real character, doing the right thing, even when no one's watching. That's why letters and numbers are called "characters"because they always stay the same.

People with strong values are like that too; they don't just go along with the crowd. They stick to what they believe in, to what matters, no matter what.

For the full list of character-based values used in this book, turn to page 229. Each story highlights how a president either lived up to a value—or missed the mark—and what we can learn from both the wins and the wipeouts.

This book is really about what brings us together: food, family, and a good story served warm. Whether it's the Fourth of July or just another Tuesday night, *Bite Back Better* is here to help you build memories that stick—just like melted cheese on a baking sheet.

Because let's face it: great appetizers don't just fill your stomach. They open hearts, spark conversations, and—once in a while—teach us something worth chewing on.

Special Note for Young Readers:
Think of this book as your grandfather pulling you aside to say, "Here's what I've learned, and here's what you should know too."

Some presidents were inspiring. Others... not so much. If I sound critical in some places, it's because actions have consequences, and not everyone acted with values like integrity, respect, or honesty.

What you're holding is a creative and heartfelt (and slightly cheesy) attempt to help you grow into someone who lives by the values that built this country. And if you do? You'll be the kind of citizen the Founding Fathers hoped for: self-reliant, purpose-driven, and full of character, not just opinions.

You've got more influence than you think. Now go make a snack and start something meaningful.

Paul Lloyd Hemphill
Chairman of American Education Defenders, Inc

American   **C l a s s i c**
Favorites

1. Buffalo Wings 11
2. Sloppy Joes 15
3. Loaded Potato Skins 19
4. Pigs in a Blanket 23
5. Jalapeño Poppers 27
6. Sliders (Mini Burgers) 31
7. Stuffed Mushrooms 35
8. Stuffed Potato Skins 39
9. Classic Deviled Eggs 43
10. Onion Rings 47
11. Pretzel Bites 51
12. Nachos 55
13. Meatballs 59
14. Cheesy Garlic Bread 63
15. Mozzarella Sticks 67
16. Chicken Tenders 71
17. Cheese Balls 75
18. Mac and Cheese Bites 79

Dips and Spreads

19. Buffalo Chicken Dip 83
20. Chips and Guacamole 87
21. Seven-Layer Dip 91
22. Hummus and Veggies 95
23. Salsa and Chips 99
24. French Onion Dip 103
25. Spinach Dip (Cold or Hot) 107
26. Buffalo Chicken Dip 111
27. Queso Dip 115
28. Bean Dip 119
29. Pimento Cheese Spread 123
30. Tzatziki with Pita Bread 127

Seafood Delights

31. Crab Cakes 131
32. Smoked Salmon Crostini 135
33. Oysters Rockefeller 139
34. Calamari Rings 143
35. Lobster Roll 147
36. Tuna Tatare 151
37. Shrimp Cocktail 155
38. Coconut Shrimp 159
39. Clam Chowder Shooters 163

International-Inspired Appetizers

40. Spring Rolls 167
41. Empanadas 171
42. Mini Tacos 175
43. Dumplings (Potstickers) 179
44. Bruschetta 183
45. Falafel Balls with Dip 187
46. Arancini (Risotto Balls) 191
47. Mini Samosas 195
48. Chicken Satay Skewers 199
49. Teriyaki Meat Skewers 2038

Light and Healthy Options

50. Caprese Skewers 207
51. Stuffed Mini Peppers 211
52. Avocado Toast Bites 215
53. Bonus Recipe: Fruits and Cheese Kabobs 219

Commander-in-Chef Quiz 223
Acknowledgements 228
Character-Based American Values 229
About the Author 230

BITE
BACK
BETTER

Buffalo Wings

A Game-Day Tradition

A Crispy, Spicy American Favorite
That Brings People Together

George Washington
"I won the Revolution on a wing...and a prayer."

Buffalo Wings aren't just a snack—they're a time machine. They take you back to those carefree Friday nights at the mall food court, Saturday afternoons at the arcade, and family game nights where someone always spilled the soda. For those of us who grew up in the '80s and '90s, they were part of the menu—bold, crispy, and tangy satisfaction.

Servings: 4 to 6 | **Prep Time:** 20 min | **Cook Time:** 25 min

Ingredients:

- 2 pounds chicken wings *(whole or separated into drumettes and flats)*
- 1 cup all-purpose flour *(for that crispy coating)*
- 1 tsp baking powder *(makes them extra crispy)*
- 1 tsp garlic powder
- 1 tsp onion powder
- 1 cup buffalo sauce *(store-bought or homemade)*
- 1/2 cup unsalted butter *(melted)*
- Salt & pepper to taste
- Carrot & celery sticks *(for dipping)*
- Ranch or blue cheese dressing *(your choice for dipping)*

Instructions to Bite Back Better*!*

1. **Prep the Wings**:
   Dry those wings with a paper towel, like blotting that pizza grease off a slice in the cafeteria. Toss them in the flour, baking powder, garlic powder, and onion powder—just like you'd toss popcorn at your sibling during movie nights.

2. **Fry the Wings**:
   Heat oil to 375°F (the same temperature as that sizzling backyard BBQ). Fry wings in batches until golden brown, as crispy as your favorite late-night snack run.

3. **Mix the Sauce**:
   Melt butter and mix it with buffalo sauce in a saucepan, creating a smooth, spicy nostalgia bomb.

4. **Toss the Wings**:
   Coat those crispy wings in your spicy-buttery sauce until they glisten like the perfect throwback food they are.

5. Serve with Veggies & Dressing:
Plate the wings with celery and carrots on the side (because you're an adult now and appreciate "balance"). Pair with your dipping sauce of choice—and yes, you still have to declare allegiance to Team Ranch or Team Blue Chees.

Fun Fact:
Did you know that Buffalo Wings were invented in 1964 in Buffalo, New York? They were originally a late-night snack served at the Anchor Bar—creating a recipe that quickly became a nationwide favorite.

Thematic Tie-In:
Buffalo Wings are a game-day tradition that embodies American gatherings—from family BBQs to Super Bowl parties and tailgates. Their spicy, buttery flavor reflects the bold, dynamic spirit of American celebrations.

Serving Occasions:
- Game Day Events
- Tailgates
- Super Bowl Parties
- 4th of July BBQs
- Birthday Parties

Drink Pairing: Pair these wings with...
- A cold American lager or hard cider
- Root beer floats for a nostalgic twist

Ingredient Substitution Options
- **Gluten-Free Option:** Replace all-purpose flour with rice flour or gluten-free breading.
- **Vegetarian Alternative:** Swap with plant-based chicken wings made from jackfruit or seitan.

DIY Presentation/Decorating Ideas:
Make these wings patriotic by serving them with a drizzle of red, white, and blue sauces or adding small American flags on toothpicks for visual flair.

Interactive Trivia Question:
What state is credited with inventing Buffalo Wings?
Answer: New York. Specifically, Buffalo, NY!

Ingredient Storytelling:
Buffalo Wings trace their origins to New York in the 1960s, a time when America was witnessing a wave of innovative, hearty, and shared comfort foods that would define iconic American sporting events and family traditions.

Legacy of George Washington:

He led the Continental Army to victory in the American Revolution, established the U.S. presidency with integrity and restraint, and unified a young nation by promoting national unity, avoiding foreign entanglements, and helping to lay the constitutional foundation for American democracy.

Washington's legacy is a powerful reminder that true greatness comes from character, courage, and commitment to a higher purpose.

As a young man, Washington faced failures and hardships, yet he persevered. He led with integrity, valuing honesty and accountability, even when it was difficult. He showed immense bravery, not just on the battlefield but in stepping away from power when he could have claimed more.

For a young person today, Washington's life teaches the importance of grit, humility, and service to others. Becoming a better person and a better American means striving to do what is right, leading by example, and contributing positively to your community—just as Washington did when he helped build a nation founded on freedom and opportunity.

What core value shaped his legacy?
Integrity: George Washington led with honesty and self-control. He gave up power when he could have kept it and set the example for future presidents. His integrity helped people trust the new government and believe in what America could become.
Question: Why do you think doing the right thing —especially when no one's forcing you to—is so powerful? Can you think of a time when someone showed integrity?

Sloppy Joes

Generator of Good Memories

A Messy, Delicious American Favorite

Dwight D. Eisenhower
"Psst! I don't wear a suit when feasting on my favorite dish."

Sloppy Joes are a timeless comfort food that represents American casual dining at its finest. Sweet, tangy, and savory, they're a nostalgic bite of history that feels like home on a plate.

Servings: 6 | **Prep Time:** 15 min | **Cook Time:** 20 min

Ingredients:

- 1 lb ground beef *(or ground turkey if preferred)*
- 1 small onion, finely chopped
- 1 cup ketchup
- 1 tbsp mustard
- 1 tbsp brown sugar *(for that perfect balance of sweet & tangy)*
- 1 tsp Worcestershire sauce
- Salt & pepper to taste
- 6 hamburger buns *(or toasted brioche buns)*

Instructions to Bite Back Better!

1. **Cook the Meat:**
   Heat a skillet over medium heat. Add the ground beef and chopped onion. Cook until the beef is browned and the onion is soft. Drain excess fat if needed.

2. **Make the Sauce:**
   Add ketchup, mustard, Worcestershire sauce, and brown sugar to the beef mixture. Stir until well combined and the mixture is heated through.

3. **Simmer:**
   Let the mixture simmer for 10 minutes, allowing the flavors to meld together.

4. **Serve:**
   Spoon the Sloppy Joe mixture over toasted hamburger buns.

Fun Fact: The origins of Sloppy Joes date back to the early 20th century, with variations found across American diners and home kitchens. They're a quick, easy, and comforting meal ideal for busy families

Legacy of Dwight D. Eisenhower:
He led Allied forces to victory in World War II, launched the Interstate Highway System as president, and maintained peace during the Cold War through balanced diplomacy and nuclear deterrence, promoting stability and prosperity while advancing civil rights and strengthening America's global leadership and infrastructure.

As the 34th President of the United States, he was known for his down-to-earth charm and love for simple comfort foods, including Sloppy Joes. This unpretentious favorite reflected his humble roots and connection to everyday Americans.

His love for simple dishes and commitment to practical solutions both highlighted his relatability and enduring influence.

Thematic Tie-In: The hearty, casual vibe of Sloppy Joes makes them perfect for family gatherings, parties, and barbecues. This timeless dish embodies American comfort food tradition.

Serving Occasions:

- Family Dinners
- Tailgates
- Birthday Parties
- BBQs
- 4th of July Cookouts

Drink Pairing Pair these with...

- An ice-cold root beer
- A classic American lager

Ingredient Substitution Options:

- **Vegetarian Option:** Use plant-based ground meat alternatives or lentils.
- **Low-sugar option:** Use sugar-free ketchup and reduce brown sugar.

DIY Presentation/Decorating Ideas:

- Add American flag toothpicks to each bun for a festive touch.
- Serve with a side of potato chips and pickles.

Interactive Trivia Question:

Where did Sloppy Joes originate?
Answer: They first appeared in American diners, with their signature sweet and tangy style defining comfort food for generations.

Ingredient Storytelling:

Sloppy Joes show how American cuisine combines simple ingredients and traditions to make memorable comfort food. They're a family favorite and a symbol of simple American gatherings.

Inspiration for America's Youth: Sloppy Joes remind us that even the simplest ingredients can come together to create something truly special—just like our nation. With a little spice, a lot of heart, and plenty of room for creativity, we can build a future that's as bold and flavorful as the traditions we share. Always remember, it's the messy moments that make the best memories!"

Which core value shaped his legacy?
Gratitude: Dwight D. Eisenhower never forgot the soldiers he led in World War II. As president, he often thanked others and worked to keep peace. His leadership showed that being thankful isn't weakness—it's strength that brings people together.
Question: Why do you think showing gratitude matters in leadership—or in everyday life? How can being thankful make a difference in your daily activities?

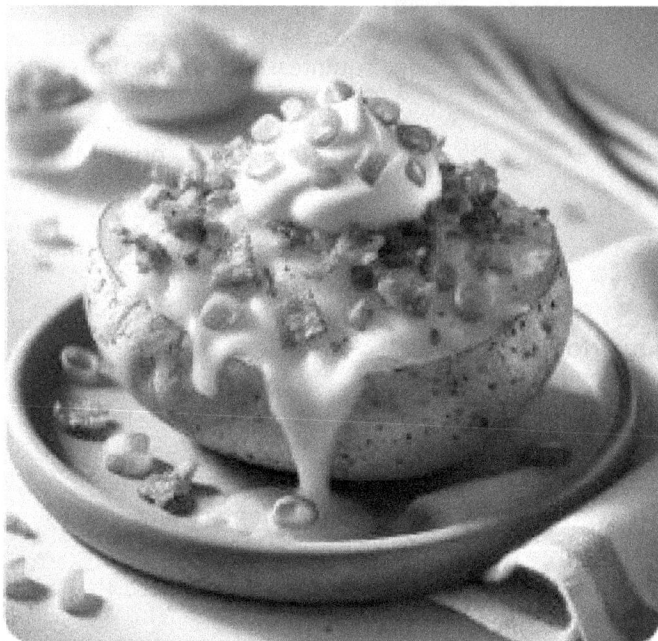

Loaded Potato Skins

A Crispy, Cheesy, and
Crowd-Pleasing Favorite

Loaded Potato Skins are a quintessential American appetizer. With a crispy shell, gooey melted cheese, smoky bacon, and zesty toppings, they bring all-American comfort and flavor to yor plate.

Servings: 8 | **Prep Time:** 20 min | **Cook Time:** 30 mi

Rutherford B. Hayes
"I once ended a political crisis, but eating these is a celebration!"

Ingredients:

- 4 large russet potatoes *(scrubbed clean)*
- 1 cup shredded cheddar cheese
- 1/2 cup cooked bacon bits
- 1/4 cup sour cream
- 1/4 cup chopped green onions
- 2 tbsp olive oil
- Salt & pepper to tast

Instructions to Bite Back Better*!*

1. **Preheat the Oven:**
   Preheat your oven to **400°F**.

2. **Prepare the Potatoes:**
   Scrub the potatoes clean and dry them. Cut them in half lengthwise and scoop out some of the flesh, leaving a thin layer of potato in the skin.

3. **Season the Skins:**
   Brush the potato halves with olive oil and season with salt and pepper.

4. **Bake the Skins:**
   Place the potato halves skin-side down on a baking sheet and bake for 20 minutes or until crispy.

5. **Add Toppings:**
   Remove the potatoes from the oven and sprinkle shredded cheddar cheese and bacon bits into each potato skin. Return them to the oven and bake for another 10 minutes, until the cheese is melted.

6. **Garnish & Serve:**
   Top with a dollop of sour cream and a sprinkle of green onions before serving.

Fun Fact: Potato Skins originated as a way to make use of potato scraps, but they quickly gained popularity as their own snack during the 1970s in the United States. They've since become a sports bar and party favorite across the nation.

Thematic Tie-In: Potato Skins are as all-American as apple pie. With their smoky bacon, gooey cheese, and crisp, golden-brown shell, they make the perfect appetizer for any celebration—tailgates, family game nights, and BBQs alike.

Serving Occasions:
- Super Bowl Parties
- Family BBQs
- Tailgates
- Birthday Parties
- 4th of July Picnics

Drink Pairing: Pair these with…
- A classic American lager
- A refreshing cola

Ingredient Substitution Options:

- **Vegetarian Option:** Leave out bacon and top with additional cheese and roasted veggies.
- **Low-fat option:** Use reduced-fat cheese and sour cream alternatives.

- **DIY Presentation/Decorating Ideas:**

- Use American flag toothpicks for a patriotic-themed party.
- Add jalapeños for a spicy kick.

Interactive Trivia Question:

Which American snack combines crispy potato skins, bacon, and cheese into one bite-sized treat?

Answer: Loaded Potato Skins!

Ingredient Storytelling:

The Loaded Potato Skins recipe reflects the creativity and versatility of American cuisine, where simplicity combines with bold flavors to create iconic comfort food.

Inspiration for America's Youth: Potato skins remind us of a simple truth: greatness often comes from humble beginnings. Like turning scraps into a nationwide favorite, your potential lies in how you use what you have. Whether it's in sports, school, or life, remember that creativity and effort can transform the ordinary into something extraordinary. Stay bold, stay inspired, and make your mark—just like this all-American classic!

The Legacy of Rutherford B. Hayes:

He may not be widely celebrated, but his legacy quietly models the kind of integrity young people can admire and follow. He became president after one of the most contested elections in U.S. history and chose national healing over political revenge. His decision to end Reconstruction was aimed at calming a fractured country, showing that leadership sometimes means prioritizing peace over popularity.

Hayes was a firm believer in fairness. He championed civil service reform, insisting that government jobs be awarded by merit, not political connections—an example of standing up for what's right, even when it's not easy.

He valued education and lived with personal discipline, avoiding alcohol and living out his principles with humility. Hayes reminds young people that character isn't about spotlight moments; instead, it's about consistent, quiet strength. He proved that real character can be measured in calm choices, moral clarity, and a commitment to fairness.

What Core Value Shaped His Legacy?
Honesty – Rutherford B. Hayes became president after a very close and controversial election. Even with the pressure, he led with honesty and pushed for fair government. He worked to rebuild trust when people had lost faith in their leaders.
Question: Why is being honest important when people are unsure who to trust? Can you think of a time when being honest made a difference?

Pigs in a Blanket

A Classic All-American Appetizer

Blanket are the ultimate American comfort food, combining simple ingredients into a delicious, flaky treat. They're great for parties, gatherings, or anytime you need a nostalgic snack.

Servings: 8 | **Prep Time:** 10 min | **Cook Time:** 20 min

George W. Bush
"I handle pigs in a blanket like I handle terrorists - decisively!"

Ingredients:

- 1 package of cocktail sausages (mini hot dogs)
- 1 package refrigerated crescent roll dough
- 1 tsp mustard (optional)
- Cooking spray or olive oil for greasing

Instructions to Bite Back Better!

1. **Preheat the Oven:**
   Preheat your oven to **375°F**.

2. **Prepare the Dough:**
   Unroll the crescent roll dough and separate it into triangles.

3. **Wrap the Sausages:**
   Place a cocktail sausage on each crescent roll triangle. If desired, add a small amount of mustard to the dough before rolling.

4. **Wrap & Seal:**
   Wrap the dough around each sausage, ensuring the ends are sealed to keep them closed while baking.

5. **Bake:**
   Place the wrapped sausages on a greased baking tray and bake for **20 minutes**, or until golden brown.

6. **Serve Warm:**
   Remove from oven and serve hot with your favorite dipping sauces.

Fun Fact: Pigs in a Blanket have been a staple in American parties and gatherings since the 1950s. Their simplicity, versatility, and comfort-food vibes make them a timeless favorite.

Thematic Tie-In: These tasty treats embody American tradition and the idea of simple, homemade comfort. Perfect for patriotic parties and casual game nights, they bring smiles and delicious memories.

Serving Occasions:

- Family Parties
- Super Bowl Parties
- Fourth of July Events
- Tailgates

Drink Pairing: Pair these with...

- A fizzy root beer
- An ice-cold cola

Ingredient Substitution Options:

- **Vegetarian Option:** Replace cocktail sausages with veggie dogs.
- **Whole wheat crescent rolls** for a healthier twist.

DIY Presentation/Decorating Ideas:

- Add American flag dipping cups with ketchup or mustard.

Interactive Trivia Question:

What American appetizer features mini hot dogs wrapped in golden, flaky dough?
Answer: Pigs in a Blanket!

Ingredient Storytelling:

A symbol of American creativity and tradition, Pigs in a Blanket represent how simplicity can lead to timeless favorites. They embody gatherings, family memories, and comfort food joy.

George W. Bush, the 43rd President of the United States, was known for his down-to-earth demeanor and steady leadership during times of crisis.

While his Texan charm and love of simple, hearty meals reflected his relatability, his legacy is defined by three pivotal achievements: guiding the nation through the aftermath of 9/11, creating the Department of Homeland Security to strengthen national defense, and launching PEPFAR, a groundbreaking global health initiative to combat HIV/AIDS.

These accomplishments underscore his dedication to security, resilience, and humanitarian efforts.

Legacy of George W. Bush:

As the 43rd president of the United States, George W. Bush's story offers teens valuable lessons in resilience and leadership. Faced with challenges like 9/11, he responded with strength and determination, showing the importance of staying calm in adversity. His initiatives, such as PEPFAR, demonstrate that even a single action can save millions of lives, inspiring teens to take meaningful steps to help others.

Despite his high position, Bush's relatable demeanor reminds young people that **authenticity** - just being who you are and not a phony - is key to earning trust and respect. His legacy highlights the power of balancing strength with compassion, encouraging young leaders to focus on making a positive impact.

What Core Value Shaped His Legacy?
Resolve – After the 9/11 attacks, George W. Bush stayed calm and determined during a time of crisis. He made tough decisions and stayed focused on protecting the country. His strong resolve showed how leaders can stand firm when things feel uncertain or scary.
Question: Can you think of a time when you had to stay strong during a tough situation? What helped you keep going?

Jalapeno Poppers

A Zesty Bite of Heat
and Flavor in Every Bite

James K. Polk
"I invaded Mexico and discovered Jalapeño Poppers!"

Jalapeño Poppers are the perfect appetizer for spice lovers. Stuffed with cream cheese, wrapped in crispy bacon, and baked to perfection, they're a combination of bold flavors and American game-day tradition.

Servings: 8 | **Prep Time:** 25 min | **Cook Time:** 20 min

Ingredients:

- 8 oz cream cheese *(softened)*
- 1 cup shredded cheddar cheese
- 8 slices bacon *(cut in half)*
- 1 tsp garlic powder
- Salt & pepper to taste(
- 8 fresh Jalapeño Poppers halved, seeds removed)

Instructions to Bite Back Better*!*

1. **Preheat the Oven:**
   Preheat your oven to 375°F.

2. **Prepare the Filling:**
   In a mixing bowl, combine cream cheese, shredded cheddar, garlic powder, salt, and pepper.

3. **Stuff the Jalapeños:**
   Fill each jalapeño half with the cream cheese mixture, pressing the filling into place.

4. **Wrap with Bacon:**
   Wrap each stuffed jalapeño half with a slice of bacon (use toothpicks if necessary to secure).

5. **Bake the Poppers:**
   Place them on a baking sheet and bake for **20 minutes**, or until the bacon is crispy and the peppers are tender.

6. **Serve Hot:**
   Remove from oven, let cool slightly, and serve immediately with ranch dressing for dipping.

Fun Fact: Jalapeño Poppers are a Tex-Mex favorite that gained national popularity in the United States during the late 20th century. They combine Mexican spice with American comfort food traditions.

Thematic Tie-In: These spicy snacks represent the American spirit—bold, flavorful, and a bit adventurous. Perfect for game days, barbecues, or any patriotic celebration, they spice up gatherings and create unforgettable moments.

Serving Occasions:

- Super Bowl Parties
- Barbecues
- Fourth of July Cookouts
- Family Game Nights

Drink Pairing: Pair these with...

- A cold American lager
- A classic margarita

Ingredient Substitution Options:

- **Vegetarian Option:** Use vegetarian cream cheese and wrap with veggie bacon alternatives.
- **Mild Option:** Substitute jalapeños with banana peppers for a less intense heat.

DIY Presentation/Decorating Ideas:

- Add American flags as toppers for a patriotic twist.

Interactive Trivia Question:

Which American appetizer combines spice, cream cheese, and bacon for a perfect bite? I know...dumb question.

Ingredient Storytelling:

The story of Jalapeño Poppers mirrors the melting pot of American culture—mixing influences (Mexican spices + American barbecue style) to create something uniquely unforgettable.

Inspiration Moment: Jalapeño Poppers are more than just spicy snacks—they symbolize bold choices, courage, and the idea that the best things in life come with a little heat and a lot of heart. They align with the journey of our youth as they learn to believe in themselves and their country, one bold bite at a time.

Legacy of James K. Polk:
As the 11th President of the United States, he showed how focus, determination, and a clear vision can lead to amazing achievements—even in a short time. During his four-year term, Polk proved that with a plan and hard work, you can make a real difference.

First, Polk negotiated the Oregon Treaty, securing the Pacific Northwest and setting the 49th parallel as the boundary with Britain. This teaches teens the value of diplomacy and standing firm for what you believe in.

Second, through the Mexican-American War, he expanded the U.S. by acquiring California, Arizona, New Mexico, and more. He believed in the nation's potential to grow, showing that *having big dreams* and the courage to pursue them can create lasting change.

Lastly, Polk's economic reforms stabilized the country's finances by reducing tariffs and creating an independent treasury system. His actions highlight the importance of setting up a strong foundation—whether for a nation, a school project, or personal goals.

The young can learn from Polk's focused leadership and his ability to set and achieve ambitious goals. His legacy is a reminder that with vision, persistence, and a little bit of grit, you can make a lasting impact on the world around you.

What Core Value Shaped His Legacy?
Focus: James K. Polk didn't try to do everything. He picked a few big goals—like expanding the country and improving trade—and stayed locked in until he got them done. He showed that real results come from staying focused and following through.
Question: Have you ever set a goal and reached it by staying focused? What helped you stick with it?

Sliders
The All-American Bite-Sized Burger

Mini Burgers with
Maximum Flavor

Sliders are the quintessential American appetizer, combining the savory taste of a juicy burger with simplicity and convenience. Perfect for parties, tailgates, or any casual gathering.

Servings: 12 | **Prep Time**: 20 min | **Cook Time**: 15 min

Calvin Coolidge
"I may be Silent Cal, but I can make these sliders disappear quickly!"

Ingredients:

- 1 lb ground beef *(80/20 lean-to-fat ratio)*
- 12 slider buns *(small and soft)*
- 1 tbsp Worcestershire sauce
- 1/2 cup cheddar cheese slices *(or your choice)*
- 1 tsp garlic powder
- 1/4 cup ketchup
- 1/4 cup mustard
- Salt & pepper to taste

Instructions to Bite Back Better!

1. **Preheat the Grill/Pan:**
   Preheat your grill or a skillet to medium-high heat.

2. **Mix the Meat:**
   In a large mixing bowl, combine ground beef with Worcestershire sauce, garlic powder, salt, and pepper.

3. **Form the Patties:**
   Divide the meat into 12 equal portions and shape them into small, flat patties.

4. **Cook the Patties:**
   Grill or cook each patty for 3–4 minutes per side, adding a slice of cheddar cheese on top during the last minute of cooking.

5. **Toast the Buns:**
   Toast slider buns on the grill or in a skillet until lightly golden brown.

6. Assemble the Sliders:
Place each cooked patty on the bottom half of a toasted bun. Add ketchup and mustard to taste and top with the other bun half.

Fun Fact: The first hamburger sliders gained popularity in diners and bars during the early 20th century. They're small in size but big on flavor—making them an American classic.

Thematic Tie-In: These sliders symbolize the heart of American cooking: simple ingredients creating unforgettable flavors. Sliders are versatile, easy to customize, and always a crowd favorite.

Serving Occasions:

- Tailgates
- Birthday Parties
- Family BBQs
- Fourth of July Celebrations

Drink Pairing: Pair these with...

- A classic American pale ale
- A fizzy cola

Ingredient Substitution Options:

- **Vegetarian Option:** Replace beef with veggie patties or black bean patties.
- **Cheese Variation:** Try pepper jack, Swiss, or gouda.

DIY Presentation/Decorating Ideas:

- Use small American flag toothpicks as toppers to show patriotic pride.

Interactive Trivia Question:

What American classic combines a juicy mini burger with the simplicity of comfort food?
Answer: Classic Sliders!

Ingredient Storytelling:

The slider represents American ingenuity—simple, versatile, and delicious. A bit of creativity with just a few ingredients can make the ultimate comfort food.

Inspiration Moment: Classic Sliders are the embodiment of American comfort food. They bring people together, celebrate great moments, and make any gathering a whole lot tastier.

Calvin Coolidge's Legacy:

Calvin Coolidge, the 30th President of the United States, may not be as well-known as some other presidents, but his achievements offer valuable lessons for teens today. Known for his integrity, humility, and strong work ethic, Coolidge demonstrated that quiet strength and consistency can lead to great success.

One of Coolidge's significant achievements was his role in restoring public trust in the government after the scandals of the previous administration. His honesty and commitment to ethical leadership helped rebuild the nation's confidence. Teens can learn from this by always striving to be trustworthy and leading by example in their own circles.

Another accomplishment was his dedication to economic stability. Coolidge promoted policies that led to economic growth, including reducing the national debt and balancing the federal budget. His focus on financial responsibility teaches teens the importance of managing resources wisely, whether it's money, time, or energy.

Coolidge's belief in the power of hard work was a hallmark of his character. He famously said, "Nothing in this world can take the place of persistence." Teens can apply this mindset to their studies, sports, or any challenges they face by staying focused and not giving up when things get tough.

By embracing Coolidge's values of persistence, integrity, and responsibility, our youth can become better individuals and contribute positively to their communities, showing that even quiet leadership can make a big impact. Check out page 162.

What Core Value Shaped His Legacy?
Responsibility: Calvin Coolidge didn't try to be flashy or popular. He believed a good leader should be careful, follow the rules, and not waste time or money. He proved that doing your job quietly and responsibly can still make a big difference.
Question: Why do you think being responsible is sometimes harder than being popular? Can you think of a time when someone showed responsibility even when no one was watching?

Stuffed Mushrooms

A Classic American Comfort With A Twist

Cheesy, Savory, and
Perfect for Any Gathering

Classic Stuffed Mushrooms have the perfect bite-sized flavor with all-American charm. They're a celebration of good times, shared memories, and deliciousness.

Servings: 8 | **Prep Time:** 20 min | **Cook Time:** 25 min

Franklin Pierce
"I got the Gadsden Purchase. Now I got these mushrooms!"

Ingredients:

- 16 large fresh mushrooms *(cleaned and stems removed)*
- 1/2 cup cream cheese *(softened)*
- 1/2 cup shredded cheddar cheese
- 1/4 cup grated Parmesan cheese
- 1/4 cup breadcrumbs
- 2 cloves garlic, minced
- 2 tbsp unsalted butter *(melted)*
- 1 tsp dried parsley
- 1/2 tsp black pepper

Instructions to Bite Back Better!

1. **Preheat Your Oven:**
   Preheat to 375°F.

2. **Prepare the Filling:**
   In a mixing bowl, combine cream cheese, shredded cheddar, Parmesan cheese, breadcrumbs, minced garlic, melted butter, parsley, and black pepper. Stir until smooth and well mixed.

3. **Stuff the Mushrooms:**
   Take each mushroom cap and fill with the prepared mixture, pressing the filling in so it holds its shape.

4. **Place on a Baking Sheet:**
   Arrange stuffed mushrooms evenly on a greased baking sheet.

5. **Bake:**
   Bake for 20-25 minutes, or until the mushrooms are tender and the filling is golden and bubbly.

6. **Serve Warm & Cheesy:**
   Remove from the oven and let them cool slightly before serving.

Fun Fact: Stuffed mushrooms have been a popular appetizer in American households since the mid-20th century. Combining simple ingredients like cheese and breadcrumbs with the natural umami of mushrooms, they quickly became an American classic.

Thematic Tie-In: Stuffed Mushrooms symbolize the warmth of home-cooked meals and family traditions. Just like every mushroom stuffed with care and love, every young person can achieve greatness when they're given the right ingredients—belief, guidance, and encouragement.

Serving Occasions:

- Holiday Dinners
- Family BBQs
- Super Bowl Parties
- Birthday Gatherings

Drink Pairing: Pair these with...

- A smooth Chardonnay
- A fizzy ginger ale

Ingredient Substitution Options:

- **Vegan Option:** Swap cream cheese and cheddar with plant-based alternatives for a dairy-free option.
- **Add-Ons:** For an extra kick, add a pinch of red pepper flakes or cooked bacon bits.

DIY Presentation/Decorating Ideas:

- Garnish with fresh parsley or chives for a pop of color.
- Serve on a platter with an American flag theme—perfect for patriotic parties.

Interactive Trivia Question:

Which classic American appetizer combines cheese, mushrooms, and comfort into one irresistible bite?
Answer: Stuffed Mushrooms!

Ingredient Storytelling:

Stuffed Mushrooms are a symbol of family traditions and American comfort food. Passed down from generations and served at countless gatherings, they remind us of gathering with loved ones.

Legacy of Franklin Pierce:
As the 14th U.S. President, he had notable achievements, including the **Gadsden Purchase**, which expanded U.S. territory in present-day Arizona and New Mexico, paving the way for a southern transcontinental railroad. He also worked to expand U.S. influence abroad, opening trade with Japan and promoting American interests in Central America. Under his leadership, the nation experienced economic growth during westward expansion, demonstrating his ability to guide the country through change.

Pierce's legacy is also marked by tragedy and struggle. He lost all three of his children, including his youngest son in a horrific accident just before his inauguration. His support of the Kansas-Nebraska Act deepened national divides over slavery, overshadowing his achievements.

Young people can learn from Pierce's story the importance of resilience, setting goals for the greater good, and seeking support when life gets tough. His life reminds us that perseverance and a focus on positive impact can help navigate even the darkest times.

What Core Value Shaped His Legacy?
Sincerity: Franklin Pierce cared deeply about the people and the pain of a divided nation. Even though his decisions didn't always help, he acted with sincere intentions and a heavy heart. His story reminds us that caring isn't always enough—character needs courage too.
Question: Can someone be sincere and still make mistakes? Why is it important to match good intentions with wise choices?

Cheese-Stuffed Potato Skins

A Crispy Cheesed
Irresistible Favorite

Cheese-Stuffed Potato Skins are the perfect appetizer to gather friends and family. Crispy on the outside, gooey on the inside, and topped with cheddar, they're a classic American comfort food that never fails to delight.

Servings: 6-8 | **Prep Time:** 20 min | **Cook Time**: 25 min

Lyndon Johnson
"I passed the Civil Rights Act, and these potato skins unite us all! "

Ingredients:

- 4 large russet potatoes *(washed and scrubbed)*
- 1 cup shredded cheddar cheese
- 1/2 cup cooked and crumbled bacon
- 1/2 cup sour cream *(for dipping)*
- 2 tbsp olive oil
- 1 tsp garlic powder
- Salt and pepper to taste
- Green onions for garnish (optional)

Instructions to Bite Back Better*!*

1. **Preheat the Oven:**
   Preheat your oven to 400°F.

2. **Bake the Potatoes:**
   Place the potatoes on a baking sheet and bake for 45 minutes, or until tender.

3. **Prepare the Potato Skins:**
   Once cool enough to handle, cut each potato in half lengthwise. Scoop out most of the potato, leaving about 1/4 inch of potato attached to the skin.

4. **Season the Skins:**
   Brush the insides with olive oil and sprinkle with garlic powder, salt, and pepper.

5. **Stuff with Cheese & Bacon:**
   Fill each potato skin with a generous amount of shredded cheddar cheese and crumbled bacon.

6. Bake Again:
Return the stuffed potato skins to the oven and bake for an additional **20 minutes**, or until the cheese is bubbly and melted.

7. Garnish & Serve:
Remove from the oven and top with green onions if desired. Serve with a side of sour cream for dipping.

Fun Fact: Potato Skins were first popularized in the 1970s as a way to make use of leftover potato parts. Since then, they've become a staple at parties, pubs, and family gatherings all across America.

Thematic Tie-In: These cheese-stuffed potato skins represent comfort, home, and family—much like how young Americans can find pride and strength in connecting with their roots and finding joy in simple traditions.

Serving Occasions:

- Football Sundays
- Family Movie Nights
- Fourth of July BBQs
- Birthday Parties

Drink Pairing:

- **Adults:** A cold lager
- **Kids:** A sparkling apple cider

Inspiration comes in all forms—even in the form of cheese-stuffed potato skins, which remind us how unity and shared experiences build stronger connections. Here's how teens can relate:

- **Game Night Fuel:** Sharing a plate of cheesy potato skins during a trivia showdown or movie marathon proves that the best moments happen when everyone comes together.

- **Potluck Power:** These potato skins always shine at a potluck, showing how everyone's contribution can create something unforgettable.

- **Cooking Together:** Making this dish with friends or family inspires teamwork and creativity, turning simple moments into cherished traditions.

Lyndon Johnson's Legacy:
As the 36th President of the United States, Lyndon B. Johnson achieved milestones that still exist. His most defining was the **Civil Rights Act of 1964**, which outlawed discrimination based on race, color, religion, sex, or national origin. Teens can draw inspiration from his courage in standing for equality, even in the face of resistance.

His **Great Society** initiative aimed to eliminate poverty and racial injustice. While well-intentioned, programs like **AFDC** (aka Welfare) were criticized for creating dependence and weakening family stability. In contrast, lasting efforts like **Medicare, Medicaid,** and **Head Start** uplifted vulnerable communities. Teens can learn from Johnson's compassion and his drive to create opportunity—but must also weigh long-term impact.

Johnson's education reforms, such as the **Elementary and Secondary Education Act**, initiated federal funding—but also mismanagement, over-standardization, and a decline in creativity, critical thinking, and test scores. His legacy teaches teens the importance of having "Plan B" - keeping alternatives available in advance in case your original plan fails. **Homeschooling** and **charter schools**, seen today as "Plan B," have proven to be effective.

In the end, Johnson's presidency reminds youth that **good intentions aren't enough**—they must be paired with results and accountability. His programs, though visionary, often lacked oversight, leading to inefficiency that still challenges the structures of our government programs today.

What Core Value Shaped His Legacy?
Determination: Lyndon B. Johnson pushed hard to pass major civil rights laws and fight poverty. His intentions were bold and often noble, though not all turned out as planned. His story shows that determination matters, but results and wisdom matter too.
Question: Have you ever tried to do something good, but it didn't go the way you hoped? What did you learn from it?

Classic Deviled Eggs
A Timeless American Starter

Creamy, Tangy, and Always
a Crows Favorite

Deviled Eggs are a quintessential appetizer that's been delighting American tables for generations. Perfectly seasoned with a little tang, they pair perfectly with a patriotic celebration.

Servings: 6-8 | **Prep Time**: 20 min | **Cooking Time**: 10 min

Andrew Jackson
"I killed the national bank, but I made deviled eggs!"

Ingredients:

- 12 large eggs *(hard-boiled)*
- 1/2 cup mayonnaise
- 1 tsp yellow mustard
- 1 tsp apple cider vinegar
- Salt and pepper to taste
- Paprika for garnish
- Chives for garnish (optional)

Ingredients

1. **Hard Boil the Eggs:**
   Boil the eggs for 10 minutes. Remove and place them into an ice bath until cool.

2. **Peel and Halve:**
   Peel the eggs, then cut them in half lengthwise. Carefully remove the yolks and place them in a bowl.

3. **Make the Filling:**
   In a large bowl, mix the egg yolks, mayonnaise, mustard, apple cider vinegar, and season with salt and pepper.

4. **Stuff the Egg Whites:**
   Pipe or spoon the yolk mixture back into the egg white halves.

5. **Garnish & Serve:**
   Sprinkle paprika and optionally chives over the top.

Fun Fact: Deviled Eggs date back to the Roman Empire but became an American potluck staple in the 20th century. They're a perfect appetizer that's both nostalgic and classic.

Thematic Tie-In: Much like the simplicity of deviled eggs, the journey of believing in yourself begins with small but impactful steps. Every bite here symbolizes resilience and history.

Serving Occasions:

- Family reunions
- Holiday celebrations
- Barbecues
- Game Day

Drink Pairing: Pair with...

- White wine
- Lemonade

Inspiration for America's Youth: Deviled Eggs remind us that the simple joys of tradition and food can build connections. Encouraging youth to believe in tradition, and community can foster hope and unity.

Fun Question and Answer:
Why don't deviled eggs ever tell secrets? Because they might crack under.

Andrew Jackson's Legacy: As the 7th President of the United States, he left a lasting mark on American history through his achievements and controversies. Known as a champion of the "common man," he worked to expand voting rights, making politics more accessible to all white men, not just property owners. This shift redefined the presidency by prioritizing the interests of ordinary citizens and marked the rise of populism.

Jackson's fight against the Second Bank of the United States was another defining moment of his presidency. Believing the bank gave too much power to wealthy elites, he vetoed its rechartering and moved federal funds to smaller state banks. While this decision reshaped the economy, it was highly controversial and sparked debates over its long-term effects.

Before his presidency, Jackson gained fame as a military leader in the War of 1812, most notably with his victory at the Battle of New Orleans. This decisive win against the British boosted national pride and solidified his reputation as a strong leader.

Jackson's presidency is also remembered for the Indian Removal Act of 1830, which forced Native American tribes to leave their lands for western territories. The Trail of Tears, one of the most tragic outcomes, led to the deaths of an estimated 15,000 to 20,000 Native Americans due to disease, starvation, and exposure. The Cherokee and other tribes, including the Choctaw, Creek, Seminole, and Chickasaw, suffered immense losses during these forced relocations.

Jackson's legacy remains complex. While he is celebrated for empowering everyday citizens and his military success, his policies, particularly those affecting Native Americans, caused widespread suffering and left a dark chapter in American history.

Young people can learn from Jackson's determination and ability to stand up for what he believed in, proving that leadership comes from action, not privilege; however, his harmful policies challenges young people to make bold choices while considering their lasting impact.

What Core Value Shaped His Legacy?
Perseverance: Andrew Jackson was known for never giving up. From surviving poverty and war to fighting for what he believed in, he pushed forward no matter the cost. But his determination also led to harmful decisions, showing that perseverance needs wisdom to be truly good.
Question: Have you ever kept going, even when something felt really hard? How do you know when to push forward and when to stop and think?

Onion Rings
Golden Loops of Liberty

A Crunchy Tribute to Freedom

These crispy, golden rings of joy are a testament to simple pleasures—just like the freedom to snack wherever, whenever!

Servings: 4 | **Prep Time:** 15 min | **Cook Time:** 10 min

Martin Van Buren
"These onion rings aren't just OK—they're my *Original Klassic*!"

Ingredients:

- 2 large yellow onions (sliced into 1/4-inch rings)
- 1 cup all-purpose flour *(the foundation of any great recipe)*
- 1 teaspoon baking powder *(for that airy crunch)*
- 1 teaspoon salt
- 1 cup buttermilk
- 1 egg
- 1 cup breadcrumbs *(patriotically panko, if you prefer)*
- 1 teaspoon paprika
- 1/2 teaspoon black pepper
- Vegetable oil (for frying)

Instructions to Bite Back Better*!*

1. **Prep the Onions:**
   Separate onion slices into rings and set aside.

2. **Make the Batter:**
   In a bowl, mix flour, baking powder, and salt. Stir in buttermilk and egg until the batter is smooth.

3. **Season the Breadcrumbs:**
   Combine breadcrumbs with paprika and black pepper in another bowl.

4. **Coat the Rings:**
   Dip each onion ring into the batter, then coat with seasoned breadcrumbs for a crunch that would make Paul Revere proud.

5. **Fry to Perfection:**
   Heat oil in a deep pan to 375°F. Fry onion rings in batches until golden brown (about 2-3 minutes). Drain on paper towels.

and became a skilled debater. As he entered politics, he saw how teamwork and negotiation could bring success.

His ability to build alliances helped him become the **8th President of the United States**. Van Buren's journey proved that with determination, sharp thinking, and strong relationships, even a small-town boy could rise to the nation's highest office.

Fun Fact: Onion rings gained popularity in the U.S. in the early 20th century, possibly first appearing in a 1933 Crisco ad. Today, they're a beloved side dish at diners and BBQ joints nationwide.

Thematic Tie-In: Each ring symbolizes unity and strength —qualities we strive to instill in young Americans. Inspire them to embrace their unique layers while contributing to the bigger picture.

Serving Occasions:
- Backyard BBQs
- Burgers and Beers Night
- State Fair Celebrations

Dip Pairing:
- Classic ketchup
- Zesty ranch dressing

Drink Pairing:
- **Kids:** Lemonade
- **Adults:** Crisp Lager

Inspiration for America's Youth: Crispy onion rings are proof that greatness comes from simple beginnings, just like our nation's young dreamers. Let this recipe remind us that every layer of effort adds up to a golden outcome!

His Legacy:
Martin Van Buren, the 8th President of the United States (1837-1841), is often remembered for his connection to the word "OK," which is one of the most widely used expressions in the world today. During his presidency, Van Buren earned the nickname "Old Kinderhook" because he was born in Kinderhook, New York. His supporters turned "OK" into a slogan during his campaign to show that Van Buren was "all correct" and fit to lead. This helped popularize the term, which had been used informally but became more widely recognized thanks to Van Buren's connection to it.

Young Martin Van Buren grew up in a small New York tavern where his parents worked hard to make a living. Listening to travelers and politicians talk, he learned how words could influence people and shape decisions. Though he had little formal education, he studied law and became a skilled debater. As he entered politics, he saw how teamwork and negotiation could bring success. His ability to build alliances helped him become the **8th President of the United States**. Van Buren's journey proved that with determination, sharp thinking, and strong relationships, even a small-town boy could rise to the nation's highest office.

What Core Value Shaped His Legacy?

Adaptability: Martin Van Buren was a skilled political thinker who helped shape the modern party system. He adjusted to changing times and built alliances to move ideas forward. But his ability to adapt didn't always lead to bold leadership when the country needed it most.

Question: Why is it important to adapt to change, but also know when to take a strong stand? Can you think of a time when you had to do both?

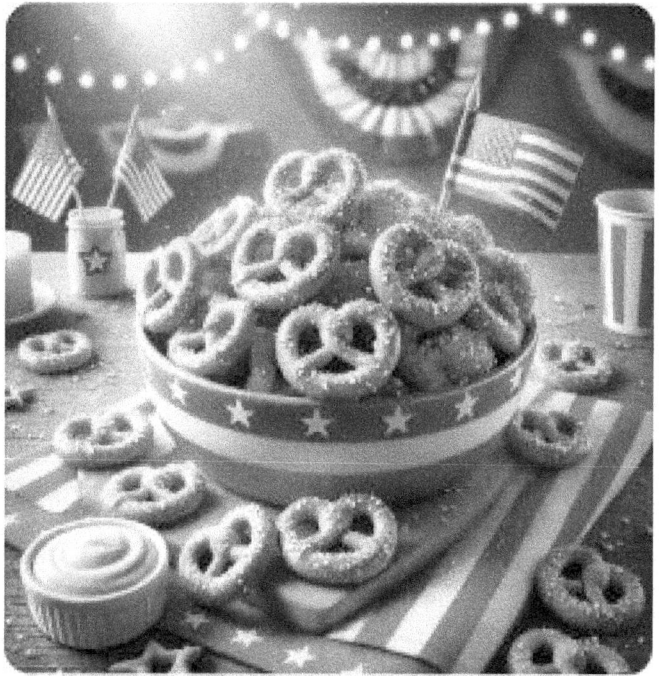

Pretzel Bites
With Cheese Sauce and Twists of Patriotism

The Perfect Snack to
Unite and Delight

Mini bites of soft pretzel goodness paired with a creamy cheese dip. They're everything we love about America—warm, inviting, and impossible to resist!

Servings: 6 | **Prep Time:** 20 min (plus 1-hour dough rise)

Cook Time: 15 min

Bill Clinton
"I've always loved a good twist since I twisted the language to define the word 'is'!"

For the Pretzel Bites:

- 1 1/2 cups warm water (about 110°F)
- 1 packet (2 1/4 teaspoons) active dry yeast
- 1 teaspoon sugar
- 4 cups all-purpose flour
- 1 teaspoon salt
- 2 tablespoons unsalted butter, melted
- 10 cups water
- 2/3 cup baking soda *(for that golden, patriotic sheen)*
- 1 egg yolk, beaten with 1 tablespoon water *(egg wash)*
- Coarse salt

For the Cheese Sauce:

- 2 tablespoons unsalted butter
- 2 tablespoons all-purpose flour
- 1 cup whole milk
- 1 cup sharp cheddar cheese, shredded *(the sharpness of freedom!)*
- 1/2 teaspoon Dijon mustard *(for a zesty kick)*
- Salt and pepper to taste

Instructions to Bite Back Better!

For the Pretzel Bites:

1. **Activate the Yeast:**
   Combine warm water, yeast, and sugar in a large bowl. Let sit for 5 minutes until frothy.

2. Make the Dough:
Add flour, salt, and melted butter. Mix until a dough forms, then knead on a floured surface for about 8 minutes until smooth.

3. Rise to the Occasion:
Place dough in a greased bowl, cover with a towel, and let it rise in a warm spot for 1 hour or until doubled in size.

4. Shape the Bites:
Preheat oven to 450°F. Line a baking sheet with parchment paper. Divide dough into 6 pieces, roll each into a rope, and cut into 1-inch bites.

5. Boil for the Finish:
Boil water with baking soda. Drop pretzel bites in for 30 seconds, then place on the baking sheet.

6. Bake to Perfection:
Brush bites with egg wash, sprinkle with coarse salt, and bake for 10–12 minutes or until golden brown.

For the Cheese Sauce:

1. Create the Roux:
Melt butter in a saucepan, whisk in flour, and cook for 1 minute. Gradually add milk, whisking constantly, until thickened.

2. Add the Cheese:
Stir in cheddar cheese and mustard until smooth. Season with salt and pepper to taste.

Fun Fact: Pretzels date back over 1,400 years and were originally shaped to resemble arms crossed in prayer. German immigrants brought them to the U.S., and they've been a snacking staple ever since.

Thematic Tie-In: Pretzel bites remind us that small efforts come together to make a big impact, just like the contributions of young patriots across the nation

Serving Occasions:

- Game Day Parties
- Movie Nights
- National Snack Day (yes, it's a thing!)

Serving Tips:

Arrange pretzel bites in a circular tray with the cheese sauce in the center—because every circle deserves a strong core!

Inspiration for America's Youth: Just like a pretzel twist, life has its challenges, or its twists and turns. This recipe serves as a reminder for young dreamers: a little effort, a lot of heart, and a dash of salt can make everything better.

Bill Clinton's Legacy:

As the 42nd President of the United States, he successfully achieved education reform, introducing programs like the HOPE Scholarship to make college more accessible and pushing for higher standards in schools. On the global stage, he led significant diplomatic efforts, such as fostering peace in Northern Ireland and the Middle East. While his presidency had its controversies, including his infamous statement about the meaning of the word "is," his achievements remain a key part of his legacy.

Bill Clinton demonstrates that ambition, resilience, and connection with people can lead to success. Coming from humble beginnings, he proved that hard work and education open doors. His focus on economic growth and education reform highlights the power of leadership, while his setbacks remind teens that mistakes don't define a person—*character does.* Clinton's ability to communicate and unite people encourages young leaders to engage, inspire, and make a difference.

What Core Value Shaped His Legacy?
Self-Control: Bill Clinton had the talent and opportunity to do a lot of good, and in many ways, he did. But his lack of self-control in his personal life hurt his reputation. His story reminds us that one bad choice can overshadow years of good work.
Question: Why is self-control important when you're in charge or setting an example for others? How can one mistake affect how people see you?

Classic Loaded Nachos
Adding Boldness and Color

Packed with Toppings

Crispy, cheesy, and packed with toppings, loaded nachos are the ultimate crowd-pleaser. Whether for game day, a family night, or a casual snack, this recipe delivers flavor in every bite. Customizable and fun to build, nachos are all about layering love—one chip at a time!

Servings: 6 | Prep Time: 15 min | **Cook Time:** 10 min

Grover Cleveland
"I vetoed more bills than any president—but I'd never veto nachos."

Base
- 1 (10–12 oz) bag of sturdy tortilla chips

Meat (Optional)
- 1 lb ground beef, chicken, or turkey
- 1 tablespoon taco seasoning
- ¼ cup water

Cheese
- 2 cups shredded cheddar, Monterey Jack, or a Mexican blend
- (Optional) ½ cup nacho cheese sauce

Toppings
- 1 cup black beans (drained and rinsed)
- 1 cup diced tomatoes or pico de gallo
- ½ cup sliced jalapeños (fresh or pickled)
- ½ cup corn kernels (fresh, canned, or frozen)
- ⅓ cup sliced black olives
- ¼ cup chopped red onion
- 1–2 green onions, sliced
- ¼ cup chopped fresh cilantro

Optional Add-Ons (After Baking)
- Sour cream or Greek yogurt
- Guacamole or sliced avocado
- Salsa or hot sauce
- Lime wedges

Instructions to Bite Back Better!

Step 1: Prep the Meat (If Using)
- In a skillet over medium heat, cook the meat until browned.
- Add taco seasoning and water. Stir and simmer for 2–3 minutes.

Step 2: Layer the Nachos

- Preheat oven to 400°F (200°C).
- On a large baking sheet or oven-safe platter, spread a single layer of chips.
- Sprinkle half the cheese, then half the meat, beans, corn, and other toppings.
- Add another layer of chips, then the remaining cheese and toppings.

Step 3: Bake the Nachos

- Bake for 8–10 minutes, or until the cheese is fully melted and bubbly.

Step 4: Finish & Serve

- Remove from oven and top with sour cream, guacamole, fresh cilantro, and lime juice.
- Serve immediately with extra napkins and big smiles.

Perfect Serving Suggestions

- Pair with Mexican rice or refried beans for a complete meal.
- Serve alongside a fresh margarita, limeade, or sparkling water.
- Great with homemade salsa or queso dip on the side.

Fun Fact

Nachos were invented in 1943 by Ignacio "Nacho" Anaya in Mexico for a group of hungry military wives. His quick thinking gave us a worldwide favorite!

Thematic Tie-In: Bold Flavors, Bold Ideas

Like the best leaders, nachos are built in layers—adding boldness, richness, and color with every choice.

Substitutions & Variations

- **Vegetarian:** Skip the meat and add extra beans or grilled veggies.
- **Spicy:** Add chili flakes, hot sauce, or sliced serranos.
- **Breakfast Nachos:** Use scrambled eggs, bacon, and cheese.
- **Dessert Nachos:** Swap chips for cinnamon-sugar tortilla crisps and top with fruit and chocolate sauce.

DIY Presentation & Decorating Ideas

- Serve on a patriotic platter with red, white, and blue napkins.
- Create a nacho bar with toppings in small bowls for guests to build their own.
- Cut parchment into stars under the chips for a themed touch!

Grover Cleveland's Legacy In 5 Pieces Of Advice:

1. Do What's Right, Not What's Easy
Grover Cleveland often said "no" to laws he felt were unfair or wasteful—even when people didn't like it. He showed that standing up for what's right is more important than trying to please everyone.

2. Think for Yourself
Cleveland made choices based on what he believed, not just what his political party told him to do. He teaches teens to trust their own judgment and not follow the crowd just to fit in.

3. Be Honest—Always
At a time when many leaders were dishonest, Cleveland built a reputation for telling the truth. His life shows that honesty builds trust and lasting respect.

4. Use Money Wisely
He believed in spending money carefully and fairly. That reminds us to be responsible with what we have and not waste it on things that don't matter.

5. Don't Quit When Life Gets Tough
After losing an election, Cleveland didn't give up—he came back and won again. His story proves that failure isn't final, and *strong character includes bouncing back*.

What Core Value Shaped His Legacy?
Integrity: Grover Cleveland didn't just tell the truth—he acted on it. He vetoed bills he believed were unfair, even when it cost him support. His choices showed that real integrity means doing what's right, not what's easy or popular.
Question: Have you ever felt unsure about what the right thing to do was? What helped you decide and how did it turn out?

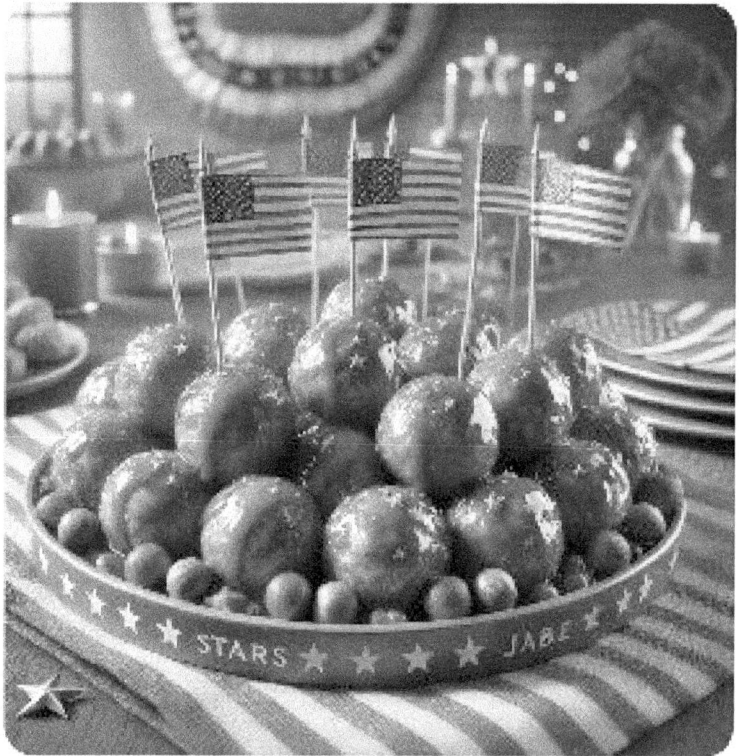

Meatballs

The Stars of the Snack Table

Round, Juicy Bites of Patriotism

Whether classic or slathered in BBQ sauce, these tender meatballs are little spheres of American comfort and joy.

Servings: 6 | **Prep Time:** 15 min | **Cook Time:** 20 min

Chester Arthur
"I reformed civil service and perfected meatballs!"

For Classic Meatballs:

- 1 pound ground beef *(a foundation of flavor)*
- 1/2 pound ground pork *(for richness)*
- 1/2 cup breadcrumbs *(the glue of greatness)*
- 1/4 cup grated Parmesan cheese *(a touch of indulgence)*
- 1 egg *(binding the dream team)*
- 2 cloves garlic, minced
- 2 tablespoons chopped parsley *(a fresh kick)*
- 1 teaspoon salt
- 1/2 teaspoon black pepper
- 1 cup marinara sauce *(a saucy finish)*

For BBQ Meatballs:

- Replace marinara sauce with:
  1 cup barbecue sauce *(sweet, smoky goodness)*

Instructions to Bite Back Better!

1. **Mix It Up:**
   In a large bowl, combine ground beef, pork, breadcrumbs, Parmesan, egg, garlic, parsley, salt, and pepper. Mix gently but thoroughly.

2. **Roll Into Perfection:**
   Form the mixture into 1-inch meatballs, each a miniature masterpiece.

3. **Sear the Spheres:**
   Heat a skillet over medium heat and add a drizzle of oil. Brown the meatballs on all sides, working in batches if necessary.

4. Simmer to Glory:

For classic meatballs, pour marinara sauce over them in the skillet, reduce heat to low, and simmer for 10–15 minutes. For BBQ meatballs, swap marinara for barbecue sauce and cook the same way.

5. Serve With Style:

Arrange on a patriotic platter and garnish with a sprinkle of parsley or chives for flair.

Fun Fact: Meatballs trace their roots to ancient Persia but have become an iconic part of American gatherings, thanks to Italian immigrants and the BBQ-loving South.

Thematic Tie-In: From potlucks to celebrations, these humble heroes bring people together with flavors that spark joy and connection.

Serving Occasions:

- Super Bowl parties
- Family reunions
- Holiday buffets

Serving Tips:

Serve with toothpicks in red, white, and blue containers for easy snacking. Add a mini flag to each meatball for a festive touch!

Inspiration for America's Youth: Like these meatballs, our youth have the power to become the centerpiece of something greater. With encouragement, they can roll into a future as strong and fulfilling as this beloved recipe.

Chester Arthur's Legacy:

Chester A. Arthur became president unexpectedly after the assassination of President James A. Garfield in 1881. Arthur had been elected as Garfield's vice president, mostly because of his connections to the Republican political machine. However, just four months into Garfield's presidency, he was shot by an assassin and died weeks later.

Many people doubted Arthur because he had been part of the corrupt "spoils system," where government jobs were given as political favors. But once in office, Arthur surprised everyone by pushing for civil service reform, signing the Pendleton Act to ensure jobs were awarded based on merit, not connections.

His presidency proved that even leaders who start with controversy can rise to the occasion and make a lasting impact.

What Core Value Shaped His Legacy?

Accountability: Chester A. Arthur entered office with a reputation for political favoritism. But once in charge, he surprised everyone. He supported reform and held himself to a higher standard. His legacy shows that taking responsibility can lead to real change—even after a rocky start.

Question: Have you ever had to admit you were going in the wrong direction and decide to do something different? What did that moment teach you about who you want to become?

Cheesy Garlic Bread
A Slice of American Greatness

Golden, Gooey Goodness

This crowd-pleaser combines rich garlic butter and oozy cheese for a warm, comforting classic.

Servings: 6 | **Prep Time:** 10 min | **Cook Time:** 12–15 min

James Buchanan
"I let the nation crumble, but at least my garlic bread stayed intact!"

Ingredients:

- 1 loaf French or Italian bread *(a crusty foundation for greatness)*
- 1/2 cup unsalted butter, softened *(creamy richness)*
- 3 cloves garlic, minced *(the flavor MVP)*
- 1/4 cup chopped fresh parsley *(fresh and bright)*
- 1 1/2 cups shredded mozzarella cheese *(for melty magic)*
- 1/2 cup grated Parmesan cheese *(for a salty punch)*
- Optional: 1 teaspoon Italian seasoning *(for extra flair)*

Instructions to Bite Back Better*!*

1. **Prep the Bread:**
   Preheat oven to 375°F. Slice the bread lengthwise, creating two halves like the Declaration of Independence ready to sign. Place cut-side up on a baking sheet.

2. **Make the Magic Butter:**
   In a small bowl, mix butter, garlic, parsley, and Italian seasoning if using. Spread this liberally on each half of the bread, ensuring every inch is covered with buttery patriotism.

3. **Add the Cheese:**
   Sprinkle mozzarella and Parmesan over the buttered bread halves. Go heavy-handed—this is no time for rationing!

4. **Bake to Perfection:**
   Bake in the oven for 12–15 minutes, or until the cheese is bubbly and golden brown, and the aroma could unite the nation.

5. **Slice and Serve:**
   Let cool for 2–3 minutes before slicing into thick strips. Arrange on a platter for maximum "oohs" and "ahhs."

Fun Fact: Garlic bread's rise in the U.S. began in the mid-20th century, inspired by Italian bruschetta and paired perfectly with American comfort foods like spaghetti.

Thematic Tie-In: This recipe embodies community and sharing—two values that make America truly strong.

Serving Occasions:

- Pizza nights
- Potlucks
- Game day parties

Serving Tips:

Pair with marinara sauce for dipping or alongside a hearty soup. Add a mini toothpick flag to each slice for a patriotic twist!

Inspiration Moment: Cheesy garlic bread reminds us of the power of unity: simple ingredients coming together for an unforgettable experience. With a similar recipe for encouragement, our youth can grow to believe in themselves and their dreams.

James Buchanan's Legacy:

As the 15th President of the United States (1857-1861), had a long and distinguished political career, serving as a congressman, senator, secretary of state, and ambassador before taking office; however, his presidency is often remembered for his failure to prevent the Civil War.

Buchanan believed that the Constitution did not give him the authority to stop slavery, even as the country grew increasingly divided. His support for the Dred Scott decision, which denied citizenship rights to black Americans, and his inaction as Southern states began to secede only deepened the crisis. By the time he left office, the nation was on the brink of civil war. He blew it. As best-selling author and historian, Bill O'Reilly said in his *Confronting The Presidents* (p 399), he was "the worst-performing president in American history."

Despite his failures, Buchanan's decades of public service are worthy of note. His legacy serves as a lesson that inaction can be just as damaging as bad decisions, reminding future leaders to stand firm in moments of national challenge.

James Buchanan's failures inspire character by showing that true leadership requires courage, responsibility, and moral conviction. His indecision in the face of crisis teaches the importance of standing up for what is right, even when it's difficult. His mistakes remind young people that avoiding problems can lead to greater conflict, highlighting the need for accountability, resilience, and ethical decision-making to create a stronger and more just society.

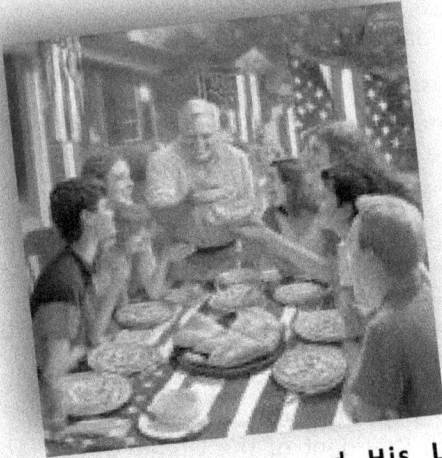

What Core Value Shaped His Legacy?

Accountability: James Buchanan avoided making hard decisions as the country moved closer to civil war. He had chances to step in but didn't. His story reminds us that avoiding responsibility can make things worse—and that doing nothing is still a choice.

Question: Why is it important to speak up or act when something serious is going wrong? What can happen if people stay silent or do nothing?

Mozzarella Sticks
Crispy, Cheesy, and Nostalgic

An Italian Influence

Crispy on the outside, gooey and melty on the inside—homemade mozzarella sticks are the ultimate snack, appetizer, or party favorite. Perfectly golden and packed with cheesy goodness, these are best served with marinara sauce for dipping!

Teddy Roosevelt
"Speak softly and carry a big mozzarella stick!"

Servings: 12 | **Prep Time:** 20 min
Freezing Time: 1 hour | **Cook Time:** 5 min

For the Mozzarella Sticks

- 12 mozzarella string cheese sticks, cut in half (for 24 pieces)
- 1 cup all-purpose flour
- 2 large eggs
- 2 tablespoons milk
- 1 ½ cups Italian-style breadcrumbs
- ½ teaspoon garlic powder
- ½ teaspoon onion powder
- ½ teaspoon dried oregano
- ½ teaspoon smoked paprika (optional)
- ¼ teaspoon salt
- ¼ teaspoon black pepper
- ½ cup grated Parmesan cheese (optional)
- Vegetable oil, for frying

For Serving

- 1 cup marinara sauce, warmed
- Fresh parsley or basil for garnish (optional)

Instructions to Nite Back Better!

Step 1: Prepare the Breading Station

- **Bowl 1:** Add flour to a shallow dish.
- **Bowl 2:** Whisk together eggs and milk in another shallow dish.
- **Bowl 3:** Mix breadcrumbs, garlic powder, onion powder, oregano, paprika, salt, pepper, and Parmesan (if using) in a third dish.

Step 2: Coat the Mozzarella Sticks

- Dredge each mozzarella stick in flour, coating evenly.
- Dip into the egg mixture, allowing excess to drip off.
- Roll in the breadcrumb mixture, pressing gently to adhere.

- Repeat steps 2 and 3 for a double coating to ensure a crispy crust.

Step 3: Freeze the Sticks

- Place coated mozzarella sticks on a parchment-lined baking sheet.
- Freeze for at least 1 hour (this prevents cheese from melting too quickly when frying).

Step 4: Fry the Mozzarella Sticks

- Heat 2 inches of vegetable oil in a deep pan to 350°F (175°C).
- Fry in batches for 30-60 seconds per side, until golden brown.
- Remove and drain on paper towels

Step 5: Serve & Enjoy

- Serve immediately with warm marinara sauce for dipping.
- Garnish with chopped parsley or basil if desired.

Perfect Serving Suggestions
- Pair with garlic knots and a side of Caesar salad.
- Serve with ranch dressing or spicy aioli for variety.
- Make it a meal by adding a side of pasta!

Drink Pairing
- **Kids:** Fruit punch or a refreshing Italian soda.
- **Adults:** A cold lager, red wine, or a classic Italian spritz.

Fun Fact

Mozzarella sticks originated from medieval France, where fried cheese became popular before spreading across Italy and the U.S.

Thematic Tie-In: Simple, Strong, and Crowd-Pleasing

Like great leadership, mozzarella sticks prove that strong foundations (breading), careful preparation (freezing), and bold action (frying) lead to amazing results!

Ingredient Substitution Options

- **Gluten-Free:** Use gluten-free breadcrumbs and flour.
- Baked Version: Bake at 400°F (200°C) for 8-10 minutes, flipping halfway.
- **Air-Fryer Option:** Air-fry at 375°F (190°C) for 6-8 minutes, shaking halfway.

DIY Presentation & Decorating Ideas

- **Patriotic Flair:** Serve on a red, white, and blue platter for a festive touch.
- **Dipping Trio:** Offer marinara, ranch, and garlic butter for variety.
- **Mini Skewers:** Serve on toothpicks for an easy party snack.

Ingredient Storytelling: A Bite of Comfort

Crispy, cheesy, and nostalgic, mozzarella sticks remind us that simple pleasures bring the greatest joy!

Teddy Roosevelt's Legacy:

He is a lasting inspiration for young people because he lived with boldness, integrity, and unstoppable energy. As a sickly child, he *chose* to become strong in both body and mind. Roosevelt believed in pushing past limits and facing challenges head-on. He was a fearless reformer, conservationist, and president who stood for fairness, hard work, and the value of nature. One famous story tells of how he refused to shoot a captured bear on a hunting trip, calling it "unsportsmanlike." That moment of compassion led to the creation of the beloved "Teddy Bear," named in his honor. Roosevelt's life teaches you to *be brave, kind, and determined,* and to lead with both courage and heart in everything you do. Roosevelt's life calls you to rise above and live with character. See a "gold" list of character development on page 164.

What Core Value Shaped His Legacy?
Perseverance: Theodore Roosevelt faced big challenges—poor health, personal loss, and political fights, but he kept going with energy and determination. He stood up to powerful industries, protected nature, and worked hard to make things better for everyday people. He didn't give up, even when it was tough.

Question: Have you ever had to keep going through something difficult? What helped you push forward instead of giving up?

Chicken Tenders
Never Out of Style!

Classic American Favorite

Golden, crunchy, and juicy— these homemade chicken tenders beat fast food any day. Perfect for kids, parties, or weeknight dinners, they're easy to make and packed with flavor. Serve with your favorite dips and sides for a classic comfort meal!

Ronald Reagan
"In America, every kid deserves a chance... and a plate of tenders."

Servings: 4 (about 12 tenders)
Prep Time: 15 min | **Cook Time:** 10–12 min

For the Chicken

- 1 ½ lbs chicken tenders or boneless chicken breasts, cut into strips
- 1 cup buttermilk (or ¾ cup milk + 1 tablespoon lemon juice)
- 1 teaspoon hot sauce (optional, for marinade)
- 1 teaspoon salt
- ½ teaspoon black pepper

For the Breading

- 1 cup all-purpose flour
- 1 cup breadcrumbs (panko or regular)
- ½ cup grated Parmesan cheese (optional, for extra flavor)
- 1 teaspoon garlic powder
- 1 teaspoon onion powder
- 1 teaspoon paprika
- ½ teaspoon salt
- ½ teaspoon pepper

For Frying
- Vegetable oil for deep frying

Instructions to Bite Back Better!

Step 1: Marinate the Chicken

- In a bowl, combine buttermilk, hot sauce (if using), salt, and pepper.
- Add the chicken strips, cover, and marinate in the fridge for at least 30 minutes (or up to 4 hours for more flavor).

Step 2: Prepare the Breading Station

- In a shallow bowl, mix flour, breadcrumbs, Parmesan (if using), garlic powder, onion powder, paprika, salt, and pepper.

Step 3: Bread the Chicken

- Remove chicken from marinade, allowing excess to drip off.
- Dredge each piece in the flour/breadcrumb mixture, pressing firmly to coat.
- Place coated tenders on a tray and let sit for **5–10 minutes** to help the coating stick.

Step 4: Fry the Tenders

- Heat 2–3 inches of oil in a deep pan to 350°F (175°C).
- Fry chicken in batches for 4–5 minutes per side, until golden brown and cooked through (internal temp 165°F / 74°C).
- Transfer to a paper towel-lined plate to drain.

Perfect Serving Suggestions

- Serve with fries, coleslaw, or mac & cheese.
- Pair with dips like honey mustard, BBQ, ranch, or buffalo sauce.
- Make it a meal with a side salad and fruit.

Drink Pairing

- **Kids:** Cold apple juice or lemonade
- **Adults:** Iced tea, lager, or a sparkling white wine

Fun Fact

Chicken tenders became widely popular in the 1980s, but similar versions go back decades—because crispy chicken never goes out of style!

Thematic Tie-In: Classic, Confident, Crowd-Pleasing

Like great leaders, chicken tenders are dependable, comforting, and always welcome at the table!

Substitutions & Variations

- **Oven-Baked:** Bake at 425°F (220°C) for 18–20 minutes, flipping halfway through.
- **Air Fryer:** Air fry at 400°F (200°C) for 10–12 minutes.
- **Gluten-Free:** Use gluten-free breadcrumbs and flour.
- **Spicy:** Add cayenne or chili powder to the breading.

DIY Presentation & Decorating Ideas

- Serve in baskets with red-checkered paper for a diner vibe.
- Offer a "dip bar" with multiple sauces in ramekins.
- Arrange tenders in a flag-shaped platter for patriotic parties.

Here are 5 character-building elements from Ronald Reagan's life, framed as quotes to inspire us all. Check out page 213 for a narrative of his legacy.

1. Optimism in Adversity
"There are no great limits to growth because there are no limits of human intelligence, imagination, and wonder."

2. Strong Communication
"Peace is not the absence of conflict, it is the ability to handle conflict by peaceful means."

3. Persistence and Reinvention
"Life is one grand, sweet song, so start the music."

4. Respect for Others
"I've always believed that a lot of trouble in the world would disappear if we were talking to each other instead of about each other."

5. Deep Conviction
"Within the covers of the Bible are all the answers for all the problems men face."

What Core Value Shaped His Legacy?

Gratitude: Ronald Reagan often spoke about how thankful he was for America and its people. He led with optimism, gave credit to others, and showed appreciation for those who served. His attitude reminded the country that being thankful brings people together—even in hard times.

Question: Why does showing gratitude matter, especially when things are tough? How can being thankful change the way people treat each other?

Cheeseballs
Golden and Crunchy

Never goes out of Style

Golden and crunchy on the outside, gooey and cheesy on the inside—cheeseballs are the ultimate snack or party appetizer. They're easy to make, easy to love, and even easier to disappear from the plate!

Servings: 20 balls | **Prep Time:** 15 min | **Chill Time:** 30 min | **Cook Time:** 5–7 min

Abraham Lincoln
"I'm dedicated to the proposition that all cheeseballs are created equal!"

For the Cheeseballs

- 1 ½ cups shredded cheddar cheese (or a blend of cheddar and mozzarella)
- 4 oz cream cheese, softened
- ½ cup grated Parmesan cheese
- 1 teaspoon garlic powder
- ½ teaspoon onion powder
- ½ teaspoon smoked paprika (optional)
- ¼ teaspoon salt
- ¼ teaspoon black pepper
- 1 tablespoon chopped chives or green onions (optional)
- ½ cup all-purpose flour
- 2 large eggs, beaten
- 1 cup breadcrumbs (panko or regular)
- Vegetable oil, for frying

Instructions to Bite Back Better!

Step 1: Make the Cheese Mixture

- In a bowl, mix cheddar, cream cheese, Parmesan, seasonings, and chives until smooth.
- Use your hands or a small scoop to roll the mixture into 1-inch balls.
- Place on a tray and freeze for 30 minutes to firm up (this prevents them from melting too quickly when frying).

Step 2: Bread the Cheeseballs

- Set up a breading station with three bowls: flour, beaten eggs, and breadcrumbs.
- Roll each cheeseball in flour, then egg, then breadcrumbs, pressing gently to coat.

- For extra crunch, repeat the egg and breadcrumb coating one more time.

Step 3: Fry the Cheeseballs
- Heat oil in a deep pan to 350°F (175°C).
- Fry cheeseballs in batches for 2–3 minutes, until golden brown and crispy.
- Drain on paper towels and serve warm.

Perfect Serving Suggestions
- Serve with ranch, marinara, honey mustard, or spicy aioli.
- Pair with veggie sticks or a salad for balance.
- Great alongside burgers or sliders at parties.

Drink Pairing
- **Kids:** Sparkling apple juice or lemonade
- **Adults:** Light beer, prosecco, or a crisp white wine like Pinot Grigio

Fun Fact:
Cheeseballs have evolved from retro party spreads to gourmet appetizers, proving that cheese never goes out of style!

Thematic Tie-In: Bold, Simple, Crowd-Pleasing
Like the best leaders and ideas, cheeseballs are small but mighty—packed with flavor and always a hit.

Substitutions & Variations
- **Spicy:** Add a pinch of cayenne or chopped jalapeños.
- **Herbed:** Mix in Italian seasoning or fresh thyme.
- **Baked Option:** Bake at 400°F (200°C) for 10–12 minutes, flipping halfway.
- **Air-Fried:** Air fry at 375°F (190°C) for 8–10 minutes.

DIY Presentation & Decorating Ideas
- Serve in a patriotic tray for holidays or themed events.
- Place on toothpicks with flags or fun labels.
- Offer a cheeseball bar with different dipping sauces and cheeses.

How Abe Lincoln Can Help With Character Development:
Abraham Lincoln's legacy offers timeless lessons in character that speak directly to the heart of today's youth. His life was built on honesty, humility, perseverance, and moral courage—qualities that shape strong and resilient individuals.

1. Honesty ("Honest Abe")
Lincoln became known for his unwavering integrity. His reputation for telling the truth—even when it was hard—teaches teens that trust is earned through consistent, honest choices.

2. Perseverance Through Failure
Lincoln faced repeated setbacks, from business failures to political defeats, before becoming president. His determination shows youth that failure isn't the end—it's a stepping stone to success if you don't give up.

3. Empathy and Unity
Leading during the Civil War, Lincoln constantly worked to heal and unify a divided nation. His compassion and deep respect for human dignity remind teens to care about others, even in conflict.

4. Commitment to Justice
By issuing the Emancipation Proclamation, Lincoln stood for what was morally right, even at great political risk. This teaches youth to stand firm for justice—even when it's unpopular.

5. Humble Leadership
Lincoln didn't seek power for its own sake. He led with humility and purpose, showing that true leadership comes from serving others, not controlling them.

His life speaks to young people: Be honest. Be kind. Be courageous. *Never give up.*

See a narrative of his legacy on page 222.

If Lincoln could speak to you right now, here's a question he might ask: **"Are you willing to do what's right, even if no one ever gives you credit for it?"**

Mac and Cheese Bites
A favorite with Kids

A Familiar Favorite with a Fun Twist

Thomas Jefferson
I wrote the Declaration,
and I declare this to be
my favorite dish!"

Crispy on the outside, creamy on the inside—Mac and Cheese Bites take comfort food to the next level. These bite-sized beauties are perfect for parties, after-school snacks, or anytime you want to serve a familiar favorite with a fun twist.

Servings: 20–24 bites | **Time:** 20 min | **Chill Time:** 1 hour **Cook Time:** 5–7 minutes

For the Mac & Cheese

- 1 ½ cups elbow macaroni
- 2 tablespoons butter
- 2 tablespoons all-purpose flour
- 1 cup milk (whole preferred)
- 1 ½ cups shredded sharp cheddar cheese
- ½ cup shredded mozzarella cheese
- ½ teaspoon garlic powder
- ½ teaspoon salt
- ¼ teaspoon black pepper

For the Breading

- 1 cup all-purpose flour
- 2 large eggs, beaten
- 1 ½ cups breadcrumbs (panko for extra crunch)
- ½ cup grated Parmesan cheese (optional)
- Vegetable oil for frying

Instructions to Bite Back Better!

Step 1: Make the Mac & Cheese

- Cook macaroni according to package directions. Drain and set aside.
- In a saucepan, melt butter, whisk in flour, and cook 1 minute.
- Slowly whisk in milk, cooking until thickened (3–4 minutes).
- Stir in cheeses, garlic powder, salt, and pepper until melted.
- Add the cooked macaroni and stir to coat.
- Transfer to a baking dish or tray, spread evenly, and chill in the fridge for at least 1 hour, or until firm.

Step 2: Shape the Bites

- Once firm, scoop and roll the mac and cheese into 1-inch balls.

Step 3: Bread the Bites

- Roll each ball in flour, then dip in egg, then coat in breadcrumbs (mixed with Parmesan, if using).
- For extra crunch, double coat with egg and breadcrumbs.

Step 4: Fry the Bites

- Heat oil in a deep pan to 350°F (175°C).
- Fry bites in batches for 2–3 minutes, until golden brown.
- Drain on paper towels and serve hot.

Perfect Serving Suggestions

- Serve with marinara, ranch, or spicy ketchup.
- Pair with a light salad or veggie sticks for balance.
- Offer on a platter for parties or movie nights.

Drink Pairing

- **Kids:** Classic chocolate milk or fruit punch
- **Adults:** Creamy stout beer, dry rosé, or sparkling water with lime.

Fun Fact

Macaroni and cheese dates back to the early 1800s and was made popular in America by Thomas Jefferson after a trip to France!

Thematic Tie-In: Small But Mighty

Like strong ideas, mac and cheese bites may be small—but they're full of warmth, strength, and satisfaction.

Ingredient Substitution Options

- **Gluten-Free:** Use GF pasta, flour, and breadcrumbs.
- **Extra Cheesy:** Mix in Gruyère or Fontina for a gourmet twist.
- **Baked Option:** Bake at 425°F (220°C) for 15 minutes, flipping halfway.
- **Air Fryer:** Air fry at 375°F (190°C) for 8–10 minutes.

DIY Presentation & Decorating Ideas

- Serve in mini paper cones or muffin liners for easy handling.
- Use flag toothpicks for a patriotic party theme.
- Arrange in the shape of a star or U.S. flag for themed events.

The Teaching Legacy of Thomas Jefferson:

Thomas Jefferson's achievements offer powerful inspiration for teens looking to make an impact today. As the principal author of the Declaration of Independence, Jefferson demonstrated the importance of using words and ideas to inspire change, even when some contradicted his own life-style. Teens can take this lesson to heart by speaking up for what they believe in, whether through writing, social media, or conversations with peers.

Jefferson's passion for learning is another valuable lesson. He founded the University of Virginia and believed that education is the key to personal and societal growth. Teens can apply this by embracing curiosity, *asking questions*, and continuously seeking knowledge—not just in school but in everyday life.

Moreover, Jefferson's vision for innovation is inspiring. He was an inventor and forward-thinker, contributing to advancements in agriculture and architecture. Teens can channel this spirit by exploring their creative ideas, pursuing hobbies, or starting small projects that align with their passions.

Finally, Jefferson's dedication to public service teaches the importance of contributing to the community. Volunteering, helping a friend, or participating in a school project are immediate ways to practice service and make a difference. By combining their voices, curiosity, creativity, and willingness to serve, teens can build a legacy of positive change—just as Jefferson did.

Buffalo Chicken Dip
The Ultimate Crowd Pleaser

Spicy, Creamy, and Perfect
for Sharing

Buffalo Chicken Dip brings the heat and the flavor to any gathering. With the perfect blend of chicken, buffalo sauce, and creaminess, this dip will have everyone reaching for chips and celery.

Servings: 8-10 | **Prep Time**: 15 min | **Cook Time**: 25 min

James Garfield
"I'm known for civil service reform—care for some dip?"

Ingredients:

- 2 cups cooked shredded chicken
- 8 oz cream cheese *(softened)*
- 1/2 cup buffalo sauce
- 1/2 cup shredded cheddar cheese
- 1/2 cup ranch dressing
- 1 tsp garlic powder
- Celery sticks and tortilla chips for dipping

Instructions: to Bite Back Better!

1. **Preheat Your Oven:**
   Preheat to **350°F**.

2. **Mix Ingredients:**
   In a large bowl, combine cream cheese, shredded chicken, buffalo sauce, cheddar cheese, ranch dressing, and garlic powder. Mix until smooth.

3. **Bake the Mixture:**
   Spread the mixture evenly into a greased baking dish and bake for **20-25 minutes**, or until bubbly and golden.

4. **Serve with Dippers:**
   Remove from the oven and serve hot with celery sticks and tortilla chips.

Fun Fact: Buffalo Chicken Dip was inspired by the flavors of Buffalo wings, combining the same tangy, spicy notes into a creamy, shareable appetizer that's perfect for any party.

Thematic Tie-In: Buffalo Chicken Dip represents bold choices, creativity, and sharing—a great lesson in teamwork and belief, much like how our youth can step into challenges with courage and community support.

Serving Occasions:

- Super Bowl Parties
- Family Game Nights
- Tailgating
- Holiday Gatherings

Drink Pairing: Pair with...

- A cold IPA
- A sweet sparkling lemonade

Inspiration for America's Youth: Buffalo Chicken Dip reminds us that bold choices can lead to wonderful results. Just as food can unite people, believing in yourself can create your own success story.

James Garfield's Legacy:
James Garfield, the 20th President of the United States, is remembered for his short but meaningful time as president and his dedication to making the country better. Even though he served only 200 days before he was tragically assassinated, Garfield accomplished a lot and left behind a lasting legacy of fairness, education, and equality.

One of Garfield's biggest achievements was standing up against corruption in government. He fought to end the "spoils system," where people got government jobs as rewards for political support, even if they weren't qualified. His efforts led to the Pendleton Civil Service Reform Act, which made sure jobs were given based on merit, not favoritism.

Garfield also strongly supported civil rights. As a former Union general, he believed in racial equality and worked to protect the rights of African Americans after the Civil War. His speeches and policies showed his dedication to making sure everyone had the same opportunities to participate in democracy.

Education was another cause Garfield cared about deeply. Coming from a humble background, he knew how important learning was and wanted to expand public education for everyone.Interestingly,

Robert Todd Lincoln, Abraham Lincoln's eldest son, was there when Garfield was assassinated. Robert, who was Secretary of War at the time, created a link between the tragic deaths of two presidents who both fought for equality and justice.

Though his time in office was cut short, Garfield's beliefs and actions continue to inspire people today.

Our youth can learn that even a short time can make a big impact if you stand for what's right. Garfield fought against corruption, promoted equality, and valued education—all things that still matter today. His story shows that **dedication and fairness** leave a lasting legacy, no matter how long you lead.

What Core Value Shaped His Legacy?

Perseverance: James Garfield rose from poverty, worked as a janitor to pay for school, and became a scholar, soldier, and president. Even after being shot, he fought to survive for weeks. His life shows that determination can carry you far, no matter where you start.

Question: Have you ever had to work hard for something when the odds were against you? What kept you going?

Chips and Guacamole
The Founding Fathers of Snacking

A Simple Yet
Revolutionary Combo

This classic dip and chip combo has been winning hearts and taste buds since the 16th century. Guacamole is the zesty declaration of independence your appetizers need!

Servings: 6 | **Prep Time:** 10 min

John Adams
"I defended British soldiers, and I'm negotiating the perfect chip-to-guac ratio!"

Ingredients:

- 3 ripe avocados *(smooth as liberty itself)*
- 1 small red onion, finely chopped
- 1 jalapeño, seeded and minced
- 2 Roma tomatoes, diced
- 3 tablespoons fresh cilantro, chopped
- Juice of 2 limes *(for that tangy zest)*
- 1/2 teaspoon salt
- 1 bag of your favorite tortilla chips

Instructions to Bite Back Better!

1. **Prep the Avocados:**
   Halve the avocados, remove the pits, and scoop the flesh into a mixing bowl. Mash with a fork until you reach your desired level of chunkiness.

2. **Add the Flavor:**
   Stir in the chopped red onion, jalapeño, tomatoes, and cilantro. Add lime juice and salt, mixing until everything is united like the 13 colonies.

3. **Taste and Adjust:**
   Taste for seasoning and adjust lime juice or salt as needed.

4. **Serve Immediately:**
   Transfer to a serving bowl and pair with crispy tortilla chips.

Fun Fact: Guacamole dates back to the Aztecs, but its first U.S. boom came after WWII, as avocados became a household staple in California. Today, it's a national favorite, especially during the Super Bowl!

Thematic Tie-In: Like the balance of creamy avocado and zesty lime, young Americans must blend self-confidence with bold ideas. Let this recipe inspire them to mix their unique talents for a flavorful future.

Serving Occasions:

- BBQs
- Taco Tuesdays
- Game nights

Drink Pairing:

Pair with:

- **Adults:** Margaritas
- **Kids:** Iced tea with lime

Inspiration for America's Youth: Every chip and dip represents teamwork, a perfect partnership for good times and shared laughs. Teach our youth the value of pairing their individuality with collaboration, creating success as smooth as guacamole.

John Adams's Legacy:
John Adams was one of America's most important Founding Fathers and a key figure in shaping the nation's early history.

As a lawyer, he showed great courage by defending British soldiers after the Boston Massacre in 1770. Though the act was highly unpopular, Adams believed that everyone deserved a fair trial, standing firm in his commitment to justice.

Adams also played a major role in drafting the Declaration of Independence in 1776, working alongside Thomas Jefferson and others to define the ideals of freedom, equality, and democracy. His passion for independence and his skill as a writer helped lay the foundation for the nation's future.

Later, as a diplomat, he negotiated the Treaty of Paris in 1783, which officially ended the Revolutionary War and recognized America as an independent nation.

Adams went on to serve as the country's second President, following George Washington. During his presidency, he focused on strengthening the young republic and keeping the nation out of war. Despite facing challenges, Adams stayed true to his principles.

In a remarkable coincidence, Adams and Thomas Jefferson, his longtime friend and rival, both died on July 4, 1826, exactly 50 years after the Declaration of Independence was adopted—a fitting end for two great patriots.

John Adams inspires young people to stand for their beliefs, even when it's difficult. His commitment to justice, education, and democracy shows that knowledge and integrity matter. He proved that perseverance and bold ideas can shape history, encouraging young people to *think independently, seek truth, and create positive change.*

What Core Value Shaped His Legacy?
Courage: John Adams stood up for fairness when it wasn't popular. He defended British soldiers after the Boston Massacre because he believed in justice for all. His courage shows that doing the right thing often means standing alone—but it's worth it.
Question: Would you stand up for someone being treated unfairly, even if it made you unpopular? What would give you the strength to do that?

Seven-Layer Dip
A Taste of American in Every Bite

A Patriotic Tower of Flavor

This dip celebrates America's diversity with seven layers of creamy, tangy, and zesty goodness—perfect for any gathering.

Servings: 10 | Prep Time: 15 min | **Chill Time:** Optional, 30 min

Gerald Ford
"I restored trust like this dip—-one layer at a time."

Ingredients:

- 1 (16-ounce) can refried beans *(the sturdy base of the dip)*
- 1 cup guacamole *(green for growth and opportunity)*
- 1 cup sour cream *(smooth and tangy unity)*
- 1/2 cup salsa *(spicy diversity in action)*
- 1 cup shredded cheddar cheese *(melty, golden Americana)*
- 1/2 cup diced tomatoes *(a pop of red vibrance)*
- 1/4 cup sliced black olives *(depth and richness)*
- 2 tablespoons chopped green onions *(a garnish of fresh optimism)*

Instructions to Bite Back Better!

1. **Layer 1:** Spread the refried beans evenly in the bottom of a glass or clear dish. This is your dip's "Constitution," holding everything together.

2. **Layer 2:** Carefully layer the guacamole over the beans, representing the lush landscapes of the USA.

3. **Layer 3:** Add sour cream for a creamy, unifying touch.

4. **Layer 4:** Spoon salsa over the sour cream. Pick a medium or spicy salsa to reflect your state's personality!

5. **Layer 5:** Sprinkle shredded cheddar cheese generously over the salsa for a golden blanket of flavor.

6. **Layer 6:** Scatter diced tomatoes across the top for a burst of patriotic red

7. **Layer 7:** Finish with sliced olives and green onions for contrast and a garnish of hope.

Serve It Up: Optional—chill for 30 minutes to let the flavors mingle. Serve with tortilla chips, pita wedges, or even fresh veggie sticks.

Fun Fact: Seven-layer dip debuted in Texas in the 1980s, originally called "Tex-Mex Dip," and has since become a national party favorite.

Thematic Tie-In: This recipe showcases how diverse ingredients come together harmoniously, just like America's melting pot.

Serving Occasions:

- 4th of July parties
- Tailgates
- Movie nights

Serving Tips:

Use a transparent dish to highlight the beautiful layers. Garnish with mini American flags for a festive look!

Inspiration Moment: This seven-layer dip mirrors life's layers—each unique, yet stronger together. Encouraging youth to believe in themselves starts with celebrating how their individuality contributes to a greater whole.

Gerald Ford's Legacy:
He was the only U.S. president who was never elected as either president or vice president.

He became vice president in 1973 when Spiro Agnew resigned due to a corruption scandal. Ford was appointed under the 25th Amendment and confirmed by Congress. Then, in 1974, after Richard Nixon resigned due to the Watergate scandal, Ford was sworn in as president.

Because he had never run for national office, he is the only person to hold both the vice presidency and the presidency without being elected to either. He later ran for a full term in 1976 but lost to Jimmy Carter.

Despite this unique path, Ford helped stabilize the nation, restore trust in government, and guide the country through economic and diplomatic challenges.

Gerald Ford inspires young people to lead with honesty, humility, and integrity. Taking office during a time of crisis, he prioritized unity over personal gain, showing that true character means making tough but necessary decisions. His willingness to heal a divided nation teaches the importance of forgiveness, accountability, and putting the greater good above personal ambition. Ford's character reminds young people that doing **what is right** isn't always popular, but it builds trust and lasting respect.

What Core Value Shaped His Legacy?
Compassion: Gerald Ford stepped into the presidency during a time of crisis and division. By pardoning Richard Nixon, he chose healing over revenge, even when it hurt his popularity. His decision showed that compassion sometimes means making hard choices for the good of others.
Question: Have you ever had to forgive someone or let something go for the sake of peace? What made that choice difficult—or worth it?

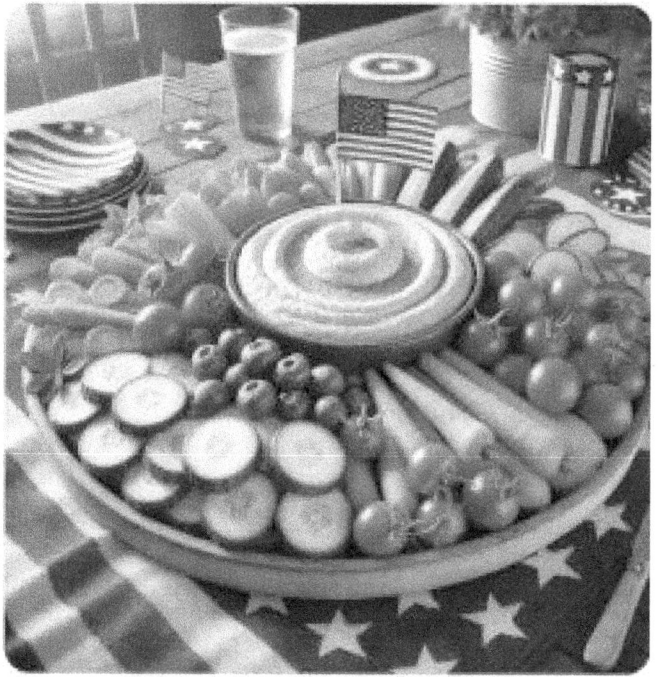

Hummus and Veggies
A Wholesome Dip for the Stars and Stripes

Healthy, Patriotic Snacking at its Best

Celebrate the vibrant simplicity of this Middle Eastern favorite paired with crisp American veggies—unity in every bite!

Servings: 6–8 | **Prep Time:** 15 min

Millard Fillmore
"I opened trade with Japan—now I'm open this hummus to all!"

For the Hummus:

- 1 (15-ounce) can of chickpeas (garbanzo beans), drained and rinsed *(hearty foundation of flavor)*
- 1/4 cup tahini *(rich, nutty undertones)*
- 2 tablespoons olive oil *(smoothness like the waves on the Hudson)*
- 2 tablespoons lemon juice *(a zesty pop of liberty)*
- 1 garlic clove, minced *(bold spice for bold ideas)*
- 1/2 teaspoon cumin *(a warm, earthy nod to perseverance)*
- Salt and pepper to taste

Veggie Dippers (Customize to your favorites):

- Carrot sticks *(orange optimism)*
- Cucumber slices *(cool resilience)*
- Red bell pepper strips *(vibrant spirit)*
- Cherry tomatoes *(burst of brightness)*
- Celery sticks *(crisp strength)*
- Broccoli florets *(green hope)*
-

Instructions to Bite Back Better*!*

1. **Blend It Boldly:**
   In a food processor, combine chickpeas, tahini, olive oil, lemon juice, garlic, cumin, salt, and pepper. Blend until smooth. Add 1–2 tablespoons of water if the mixture is too thick.

2. **Taste for Freedom:**
   Adjust salt, pepper, or lemon juice to suit your patriotic palate.

3. Plate It Proudly:
Scoop hummus into a serving bowl. Create a swirl on the surface with a spoon and drizzle with olive oil for flair. Add a sprinkle of paprika for a patriotic red accent.

4. Arrange Veggie Dippers:
Fan the veggies around the bowl like a colorful firework display.

Fun Fact: Though hummus originated in the Middle East, it's now a staple on American tables, symbolizing cultural exchange and shared values.

Thematic Tie-In: This dish represents the unity of international influences blended with homegrown traditions, inspiring young people to embrace their roots while exploring new horizons.

Serving Occasions:

- Backyard barbecues
- Health-conscious 4th of July picnics
- Study snacks for budding patriots

Serving Tips:

Garnish hummus with roasted red peppers, toasted pine nuts, or fresh parsley for extra flair. Serve with patriotic toothpicks for fun!

Inspiration Moment: A middle school teacher wanted to help her students understand the power of diversity and collaboration. She brought in a variety of ingredients—chickpeas, tahini, lemon, garlic, and fresh veggies—and asked the class to taste them individually. Some students liked certain flavors, while others found them too strong or bland. Then, they blended the ingredients together to make hummus. Suddenly, the students realized how these simple, different elements created something smooth, rich, and delicious when combined.

The teacher used this as a lesson: just like hummus, people have different strengths and qualities, and when they come together, they create something even better. This simple exercise helped students see that appreciating differences and working together leads to something greater—just like believing in oneself and others builds a stronger community.

Millard Fillmore's Legacy:
As the 13th President of the United States (1850–1853), left a lasting but complex legacy marked by his efforts to preserve the Union, expand international trade, and support America's westward growth. As president, he played a pivotal role in the passage of the Compromise of 1850, a series of laws aimed at easing tensions between the North and South. While the compromise temporarily maintained national stability, its inclusion of the Fugitive Slave Act deepened the divide over slavery.

Beyond domestic affairs, Fillmore sought to expand American influence abroad. In 1852, he dispatched Commodore Matthew Perry to Japan, leading to the Treaty of Kanagawa in 1854, which opened Japan to U.S. trade after centuries of isolation. At home, he championed infrastructure development, laying the groundwork for the Transcontinental Railroad by supporting surveys and land grants. His presidency, though often overlooked, helped shape America's expansion and global reach.

Millard Fillmore inspires young people to embrace lifelong learning, adaptability, and perseverance. Rising from humble beginnings, he proved that education and hard work can open doors. His efforts to modernize the nation, including expanding trade and supporting libraries, highlight the importance of curiosity and growth. While his presidency had controversial decisions, his story teaches young people that character is shaped by choices, and true leadership requires both wisdom and moral courage.

What Core Value Shaped His Legacy?Respect: Millard Fillmore tried to keep peace between the North and South during a time of growing tension. While not all his decisions aged well, he believed in respecting different views to hold the country together. His story shows how respect can be difficult—but necessary.
Question: How do you show respect to people you don't agree with? Why is that sometimes harder than staying silent or walking away?

Salsa and Chips
A Zesty Dip with a Crunch of Freedom

America's Favorite Snack
for Anytime Patriotism

Celebrate unity with this classic duo of bold, tangy salsa and crunchy, satisfying tortilla chips.

Servings: 6–8 | **Prep Time:** 15 min

John Quincy Adams
"I spread diplomacy like salsa—bold, zesty, and all-American."

For the Salsa:

- 4 large ripe tomatoes, finely diced *(red like the stripes on the flag)*
- 1 small onion, finely chopped *(layers of resilience)*
- 1–2 jalapeño peppers, finely chopped *(a fiery kick of independence)*
- 1/4 cup fresh cilantro, chopped *(a green flourish of hope)*
- Juice of 1 lime *(zesty brightness to shine through)*
- 1/2 teaspoon cumin *(earthy warmth for togetherness)*
- Salt and pepper to taste

For the Chips:

- 1 large bag of tortilla chips (store-bought or homemade) *(golden and proud)*

Instructions to Bite Back Better!

1. **Prep the Ingredients:**
   Dice the tomatoes, onions, and jalapeños with precision, like a founding document in progress.

2. **Mix with Purpose:**
   Combine all the salsa ingredients in a large bowl. Stir together like a melting pot of flavor.

3. **Taste for Justice:**
   Adjust salt, pepper, or lime juice to achieve balance.

4. Chill with Dignity:
Let the salsa rest in the refrigerator for at least 30 minutes to meld flavors.

5. Serve with Pride:
Pour the salsa into a serving bowl and surround it with tortilla chips arranged in a starburst pattern.

Fun Fact: Salsa became America's favorite condiment in the 1990s, overtaking ketchup—a testament to the nation's evolving taste for bold, diverse flavors.

History: Though originating in Central America, salsa has become a beloved symbol of shared heritage in the U.S., embodying the fusion of cultures that defines American cuisine.

Serving Occasions:

- Game-day gatherings
- Summer cookouts
- Study breaks with patriotic flair

Serving Tips:

Add diced avocado or a splash of hot sauce to spice things up. Pair with a side of guacamole for a double dose of deliciousness!

Inspiration Moment: Salsa and chips are a perfect pairing that represents balance, diversity, and unity. This recipe reminds young people that combining bold flavors—like blending unique qualities—creates something unforgettable, encouraging belief in their potential.

John Quincy Adams's Legacy:
History is full of people who stood up for what was right, even when no one wanted to listen. John Quincy Adams was one of them. His story isn't just something from a history book; it's a reminder that one person's persistence can spark change, even in the face of resistance. I thought about his fight when I faced a challenge of my own. To measure the legacy of Adams, let's imagine the following scenario.

"The classroom fell silent as I stood up. My heart pounded, but I knew I had to speak. The school wanted to cut funding for a program that helped students who struggled in math—kids like my best friend. I wasn't the most popular student, and I didn't have the loudest voice, but I knew that if I didn't fight for this, no one else would.

"That's when I thought of John Quincy Adams, a man who refused to back down, even when the odds were against him. After serving as president, Adams could have retired quietly, but instead, he did something unheard of—he went back to Congress. And there, he fought for what he knew was right: ending slavery.

"For years, people ignored him. Some mocked him. Others even tried to silence him completely. But he kept speaking. He kept pushing. And even though he didn't live to see slavery abolished, his fight inspired the next generation—including **Abraham Lincoln**—to finish what he started.

"So I took a deep breath and spoke. I didn't know if I would win, but I knew this: **one voice can spark change.** Adams proved it. Now it was my turn."

What Core Value Shaped His Legacy?

Service: John Quincy Adams believed in helping others through action. Even after being president, he worked in Congress and spoke out against slavery. He showed that making a difference means using your time and voice to help people—even when there's nothing in it for you.

Question: Have you ever used your time or voice to help someone else? Why do you think helping others—even in small ways—matters?

French Onion Dip
A Creamy Classic Worth Dipping For

America's Comfort Dip With
a Touch of Sophistication

Herbert Hoover
"I fought hunger—now
I'm serving dip!"

This smooth, savory delight will have your guests rallying for seconds and thirds.

Servings: 6–8 | **Prep Time:** 10 min | **Chill Time:** 1 hr (for best flavor)

Ingredients:

- **1** cup sour cream *(smooth as unity)*
- 1/2 cup mayonnaise *(the base of democracy—solid yet flexible)*
- 1 packet (1 oz) onion soup mix *(savory and seasoned like history)*
- 1 teaspoon garlic powder *(a subtle patriotic kick)*
- Salt and pepper to taste

Instructions to Bite Back Better!

1. **Blend the Basics:**
   Combine sour cream, mayonnaise, onion soup mix, and garlic powder in a mixing bowl. Stir until harmonious.

2. **Taste for Unity:**
   Season with salt and pepper as needed to ensure every bite is balanced.

3. **Chill for Harmony:**
   Cover the dip and refrigerate for at least 1 hour to let the flavors meld into a perfect union.

4. **Serve with Freedom:**
   Transfer to a serving dish, and surround with fresh veggies, potato chips, or crackers for dipping.

Fun Fact: French onion dip originated in the 1950s in California, becoming a national sensation. It was dubbed "California Dip" before being renamed for its key ingredient, French onion soup mix.

History: Born from convenience and ingenuity, French onion dip reflects the American knack for adapting global flavors into beloved classics.

Serving Occasions:

- Fourth of July parties
- Movie nights
- Post-game celebrations

Serving Tips:

Garnish with freshly chopped parsley or green onions for an elevated look. Serve alongside patriotic red and blue tortilla chips for a festive touch!

Inspiration for America's Youth: This creamy, savory dip is more than a snack—it's a reminder to bring diverse ingredients together for a stronger, better-tasting whole. Let it inspire young people to believe that their unique qualities contribute to a brighter future for all.

Herbert Hoover's Legacy:
When disaster strikes, most people wait for someone else to fix things. But not **Herbert Hoover**—he stepped up when no one else would.

Before he became president, Hoover was a humanitarian, engineer, and leader who believed in solving problems, not waiting for others to act. When World War I broke out, thousands of Americans were stranded in Europe with no money or way to get home.

The U.S. government wasn't doing anything—but Hoover didn't wait. He organized food, shelter, and travel for over 120,000 Americans, ensuring they got home safely.

Later, he tackled an even bigger crisis. Millions in Belgium were starving because of the war. Hoover, using his skills as an engineer and organizer, raised money, secured food shipments, and personally oversaw distribution, feeding an entire nation. His success earned him the nickname "The Great Humanitarian."

Then came the Great Depression. As president, Hoover created public works projects like the Hoover Dam, providing jobs and infrastructure to help struggling Americans.

Why does this matter to you? Because Hoover's story proves that *you don't need permission to make a difference.* He didn't wait—he acted. See a problem? Step up and fix it.

Here are **4 quotes** that reflect Herbert Hoover's character traits—each offering a powerful lesson for young people:

1. **Service Before Self**
   "Children are our most valuable resource."
   — A reminder that leadership means putting others' well-being first.

2. **Hard Work and Self-Reliance**
   "Be patient and calm—for no one can catch fish in anger."
   — A call to stay steady, work hard, and remain focused even in difficulty.

3. **Integrity in Crisis**
   "Honor is not the exclusive property of any political party."
   — A statement on staying true to values, even when it's unpopular.

4. **Global Citizenship**
   "Peace is not made at the council table or by treaties, but in the hearts of men."
   — A message that empathy and global understanding begin with personal growth.

These quotes reflect Hoover's quiet strength and deep belief in moral character, perseverance, and service.

If Herbert Hoover could speak to you now, how would you answer his questions?
"Are you doing something today that helps someone else before yourself? What does it look like to stay true to your values when no one's watching?"

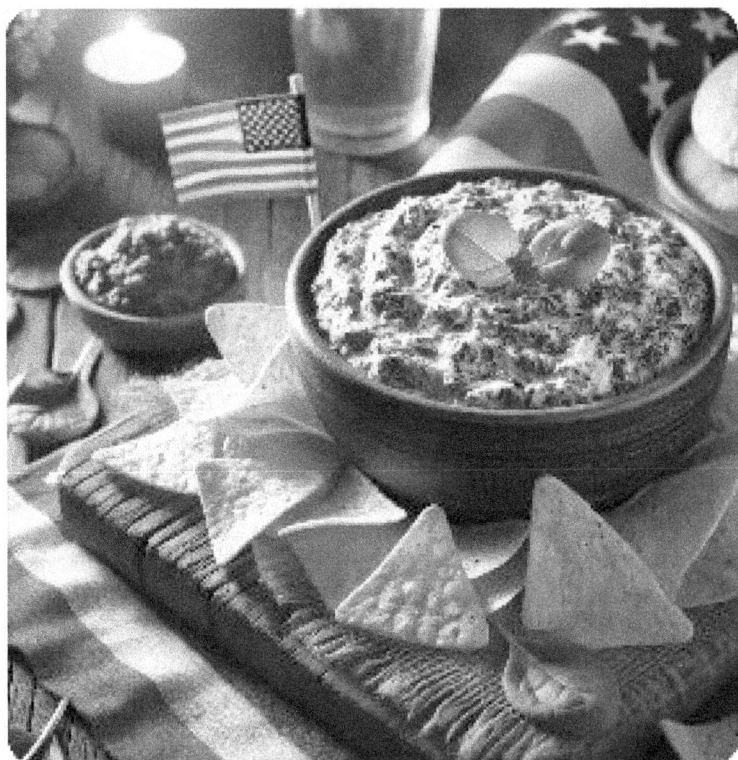

Spinach Dip (Hot or Cold)
A Dip for the Stars and Stripes

A Patriotic Classic for Pleasing Crowds

This all-American favorite combines rich flavors with the wholesome goodness of spinach, bringing everyone to the table.

Servings: 6–8 | **Prep Time:** 10 min | **Cook Time** (if served hot): 20–25 min

Harry Truman
"The buck stops here... right at this bowl of spinach dip!"

Ingredients:

- 2 cups fresh spinach, chopped (or 1 package frozen, thawed and drained) (green as the American dream)
- 1 cup sour cream (smooth and tangy as hope)
- 1 cup mayonnaise (the creamy backbone of many American recipes)
- 1 cup shredded Parmesan cheese (sharp and proudly aged)
- 1 cup shredded mozzarella cheese (gooey and unifying)
- 1 clove garlic, minced (a subtle spark)
- 1/2 teaspoon salt (to taste, like freedom)
- Optional for hot version: 1/4 teaspoon crushed red pepper flakes

Instructions (Cold Version) to Bite Back Better!

1. **Mix for Unity:**
   In a medium bowl, combine sour cream, mayonnaise, spinach, Parmesan, garlic, and salt. Stir until blended.
2. **Chill and Serve:**
   Refrigerate for at least 2 hours for flavors to meld. Serve in a bread bowl with vegetable sticks or crackers for dipping.

Instructions (Hot Version) to Bite Back Better!

1. **Preheat the Oven:**
   Set oven to 375°F, where all things come together for greatness.

2. **Combine and Heat:**
   Mix all ingredients (except mozzarella) in a bowl, then transfer to a baking dish.

3. Top and Bake:
Sprinkle mozzarella on top and bake for 20–25 minutes or until bubbling and golden.

Fun Fact: Spinach dip soared in popularity during the 1950s with the rise of party culture, often served cold in hollowed-out bread bowls at gatherings

History: This dish reflects the resourcefulness of American homemakers, turning humble ingredients into a dip that became a party staple. From potlucks to game days, it's a testament to the power of food to bring people together.

Serving Occasions:

- Memorial Day BBQs
- Super Bowl parties
- Casual family game nights

Serving Tips:

- Pair with crusty bread, pita chips, or tortilla chips for a satisfying crunch.
- Add a patriotic touch by serving with red and blue tortilla chips!

Inspiration for America's Youth: Whether served hot or cold, spinach dip proves that even the simplest ingredients can create something extraordinary—an inspiring reminder to young people that they, too, can shine with what they have.

Harry Truman's Legacy:
When Harry Truman became president in 1945, he wasn't the most popular or experienced leader. But he had one thing that set him apart—he took responsibility when it mattered most.

Truman had to make impossible choices, like ending World War II and rebuilding nations. He made the tough call to drop the atomic bomb, launched the Marshall Plan to help Europe recover, and stood firm against communism with the Truman Doctrine. Through it all, he lived by his motto: "The Buck Stops Here"—meaning he didn't pass problems to someone else.

So what does this mean for you? As a teen or preteen, you can step up—whether it's leading a group project, helping a friend, or standing up for what's right. It's character in action: taking responsibility, even when it's hard, is what makes a leader. Just like Truman, you can be that person.

What Core Value Shaped His Legacy?
Courage: Harry Truman made some of the toughest calls in U.S. history—including ending a world war and firing a powerful general. He didn't run from pressure. He faced it, took responsibility, and acted. His story shows that courage isn't about being fearless; it's about standing firm when it counts most.
Question: Have you ever had to make a hard choice, even if others didn't agree? What helped you stay strong in that moment?

Buffalo Chicken Dip
Bold, Spicy, and Unapologetically American

A Crowd-Pleaser that Soars
on Wings of Flavor

This creamy, zesty dip embodies the fiery spirit of American ingenuity and is the ultimate game-day hero.

Servings: 6–8 | **Prep Time:** 10 min | **Cook Time:** 20 min

William Henry Harrison
"I didn't last, but this Buffalo Chicken Dip sure will!"

Ingredients:

- 2 cups shredded rotisserie chicken (hearty and resourceful, like the American spirit)
- 8 ounces cream cheese, softened (a rich foundation)
- 1/2 cup buffalo wing sauce (bold as freedom)
- 1/2 cup ranch dressing (smooth as democracy in action)
- 1 cup shredded cheddar cheese (sharp and golden as opportunity)
- 1/4 cup blue cheese crumbles (optional) (for the bold risk-takers)
- Tortilla chips, celery sticks, or carrot sticks for serving

Instructions to Bite Back Better!

1. **Preheat the Oven:**
   Set to 375°F, ready to rally for a bubbling, cheesy finish.

2. **Mix It Up:**
   In a medium bowl, combine chicken, cream cheese, buffalo sauce, ranch dressing, and half of the cheddar cheese. Stir until evenly mixed, united like the states.

3. **Assemble and Bake:**
   Spread the mixture into a baking dish, top with remaining cheddar cheese, and bake for 20 minutes or until hot and bubbly.

4. **Serve with Pride:**
   Garnish with blue cheese crumbles and a sprinkle of parsley, then serve with tortilla chips or fresh veggies for dipping.

Fun Fact: Buffalo chicken dip draws inspiration from the iconic Buffalo wings, invented at Anchor Bar in Buffalo, New York, in 1964—a true American classic!

History: This dip transforms the beloved Buffalo wing flavor into a sharable dish. It gained popularity as a game-day essential in the early 2000s, proving that America excels at reinvention.

Serving Occasions:

- Super Bowl Sunday
- Fourth of July celebrations
- Backyard barbecues

Serving Tips:

- Add red, white, and blue veggie sticks for a patriotic touch.
- Use small ramekins for individual servings—perfect for a pandemic-friendly party!

Closing Thought:

Buffalo chicken dip reminds us that fiery determination and creativity can turn a simple idea into a national favorite. It inspires young people to believe that even *bold, spicy dreams are worth pursuing*.

William Henry Harrison's Legacy:

Most people play it safe, but William Henry Harrison believed in showing up and leading by example, even when it cost him everything.

Before becoming the shortest-serving U.S. president, Harrison was a fearless military leader. At just 26- years-old, he became the governor of the Indiana Territory, where he negotiated peace treaties but wasn't afraid to fight when necessary.

In 1811, he led his men into the Battle of Tippecanoe against a confederation of Native American warriors. The battle was brutal, but Harrison didn't sit back and give orders from a tent: he was on the battlefield, leading from the front. His courage won the battle and made him a national hero.

So what does this mean for you? **Character isn't about titles, it's about action**. If there's a problem at school or in your community, don't wait for someone else to step up. Be the one who takes charge. Stand up for what's right, even when it's tough. When you do that, you will be amazed at how many people will quietly look up to you.

Whether it's leading a group project, defending a friend, or starting something new, people with character, who stick to a set of values that don't change, don't just talk— they act. It's a way to define courage.

Harrison proved that showing up, taking risks, and leading from the front is what makes a difference. So **why not start today?**

What Core Value Shaped His Legacy?
Service: William Henry Harrison spent most of his life serving the country—as a soldier, governor, and leader. Though his presidency was cut short, his dedication to helping others and answering the call of duty showed that a life of service doesn't need to be long to matter.
Question: Why do you think it's important to show up and do your part, even if you don't get much time or recognition for it?

Queso Dip
The Melted Heart of American Unity

Creamy, Cheesy Goodness that
Brings Everyone to the Table

This silky, flavorful dip channels the warmth and togetherness of a nation united by food.

Servings: 8–10 | **Prep Time:** 5 min | **Cook Time:** 10 min

William Howard Taft
"I may be big, but this Queso Dip is even bigger on flavor!"

Ingredients:

- 2 tablespoons unsalted butter (the rich base of every good story)
- 2 tablespoons all-purpose flour (a sturdy framework for greatness)
- 1 cup whole milk (smooth, like a well-functioning democracy)
- 1 cup shredded sharp cheddar cheese (bright and bold)
- 1 cup shredded Monterey Jack cheese (melting pot perfection)
- 1/2 cup canned diced tomatoes with green chilies (drained) (a spicy nod to diversity)
- 1/4 teaspoon ground cumin (earthy depth, like our nation's roots)
- Salt and pepper, to taste (because balance matters)

- Tortilla chips or fresh vegetables for serving

Instructions to Bite Back Better!

1. **Melt and Mix:**
   In a medium saucepan, melt butter over medium heat. Stir in flour, cooking until lightly golden—this is your creamy declaration of independence.

2. **Create the Base:**
   Gradually whisk in milk, cooking until the mixture thickens.

3. **Cheese It Up:**
   Reduce heat to low and stir in the cheeses until fully melted. Fold in diced tomatoes and green chilies, then season with cumin, salt, and pepper.

4. Serve Warm and Proud:

Transfer to a serving dish or slow cooker set to warm. Pair with tortilla chips or fresh veggies.

Fun Fact "Queso" means "cheese" in Spanish, but its Americanized form became a Tex-Mex staple, starting with its rise to fame in Texas in the 1940s.

History: Queso dip evolved from Mexican queso fundido, a melted cheese dish, but gained an all-American twist by incorporating processed cheese and canned chilies, turning it into a quick-and-easy party favorite.

Serving Occasions:

- Independence Day cookouts
- Movie nights
- Potluck gatherings

Serving Tips:

- Keep warm in a slow cooker to avoid any "cheesy" separation anxiety.
- Add a sprinkle of paprika or fresh cilantro for a decorative, patriotic flair.

Inspiration Moment: Queso dip embodies the melting pot spirit of America, encouraging young people to embrace their roots while forging new paths. A single bowl reminds us that even diverse ingredients can come together to create something truly unforgettable.

William Howard Taft's Legacy:

William Howard Taft wasn't just the biggest president in history—he weighed 350 pounds—he made big moves that shaped America. Unlike other leaders, Taft didn't chase popularity; he focused on doing what was right.

First, he busted more monopolies than Teddy Roosevelt, breaking up powerful companies that were cheating the system. He believed that fairness in business meant fairness for the people.

Next, he expanded America's influence around the world with "Dollar Diplomacy." Instead of using war, he helped U.S. businesses invest in other countries, strengthening America's economy while keeping peace.

Finally, after serving as president, he became Chief Justice of the Supreme Court, proving that leadership isn't about holding just one title—it's about making a difference wherever you're called to serve.

So what can you learn from Taft? Don't just follow the crowd—do what's right. Lead with fairness, think big, and always look for new ways to serve others.

And yes, there's one more thing worth clearing up. Over the years, a silly myth spread about his weight—that he got stuck in a bathtub and had to be pulled out by several men. It was pure fake news. Sadly, that story stuck around far too long and distracted from the real legacy Taft left behind—as both a President and a Chief Justice who led with thoughtfulness, dedication, and integrity.

What Core Value Shaped His Legacy?
Respect: William Howard Taft believed deeply in the law and the Constitution. He respected the rules, even when politics pressured him to bend them. Later, as Chief Justice, he showed that respecting fairness and truth matters more than winning or being popular.
Question: Why is it sometimes hard to stick to what's fair when others want you to take sides? What helps you stay respectful in those moments?

Bean Dip
Spicy, Cheesy, and Smokey

Melting Pot of Flavors
that Define America

Bean dip isn't just a snack—it's a symbol of bold flavors and togetherness. Whether at a BBQ, game night, or Fourth of July party, this creamy, cheesy, and zesty dish brings people together.

Servings 8-10 | **Prep Time**: 5 min | **Cook Time:** 20–25 min

Woodrow Wilson
"I united nations—now unite over this dip!"

Ingredients:

- 2 cans (15 oz each) refried beans
- 1 cup sour cream
- 1 cup shredded cheddar cheese
- ½ cup pepper jack cheese, shredded
- 1 packet taco seasoning
- 1 can (10 oz) Rotel tomatoes with green chilies, drained
- ½ cup cream cheese, softened
- 1 teaspoon garlic powder
- ½ teaspoon cumin
- ¼ teaspoon smoked paprika
- ¼ teaspoon black pepper
- ½ cup diced green onions (for garnish)
- ¼ cup chopped cilantro (optional)
- Tortilla chips or veggie sticks for serving

Instructions to Bite Back Better!

1. Preheat oven to 375°F (190°C). Lightly grease a baking dish.
2. In a large bowl, mix refried beans, sour cream, cream cheese, and taco seasoning until smooth.
3. Stir in Rotel tomatoes, garlic powder, cumin, smoked paprika, and black pepper until well combined.
4. Spread the mixture evenly in the baking dish and top with cheddar and pepper jack cheese.
5. Bake for 20-25 minutes or until the cheese is bubbly and slightly golden.
6. Remove from the oven and sprinkle with green onions and cilantro.
7. Serve warm with tortilla chips or fresh veggies.

Fun Fact:

Did you know that beans were a staple food for early American settlers and soldiers? From the pioneers on the frontier to cowboys on the trail, beans fueled hard work and resilience—just like this dip fuels big gatherings!

Thematic Tie-In:

This red, white, and bold dip represents the melting pot of flavors that define America. Just like our nation, it blends different elements—spicy, creamy, cheesy, and smoky—to create something stronger and more delicious together.

Perfect Serving Occasions:
- Fourth of July cookouts
- Super Bowl parties
- Family game nights
- Tailgates and BBQs
- Casual hangouts with friends

Drink Pairing:

- Classic: A cold cola or root beer for a nostalgic American pairing.
- Lemonade or a lime-infused sparkling water for a crisp contrast.
- For adults: A lager beer or spicy margarita pairs well with the smoky and cheesy flavors.

Ingredient Substitution Options:

- Dairy-Free? Swap sour cream and cheese for plant-based alternatives.
- Spicier Kick? Add chopped jalapeños or a dash of hot sauce.
- Low-Carb? Serve with sliced cucumbers, bell peppers, or pork rinds instead of chips.

DIY Presentation & Decorating Ideas:

- Patriotic Platter: Serve in a blue baking dish with tortilla chips arranged in red, white, and blue sections.
- Cheese Flag: Before baking, arrange strips of cheese and a "star" of sour cream in a flag pattern.
- Mason Jar Dips: Layer the dip in individual mason jars for easy grab-and-go servings at parties!

Ingredient Storytelling:

Beans have been a symbol of strength and nourishment for centuries. From Native American stews to cowboy chuckwagons, beans have powered explorers, workers, and leaders. This dip carries that legacy forward, proving that something simple—when prepared with heart—can become truly extraordinary.

Closing Thought for America's Youth:

Whether you're working toward a dream, standing up for a friend, or bringing people together, what you contribute makes a difference. Stay bold, stay flavorful, and make your mark—one chip at a time.

Woodrow Wilson's Legacy:

In 1919, Woodrow Wilson, the 28th president and a known racist, fought to create the League of Nations, a global peace organization. But after years of hard work, Congress rejected his plan. Wilson's dismissal of the Constitution as "outdated," his suppression of free speech, his resegregation of government departments, and his expansion of federal bureaucracies are among the most damaging policies he initiated. Many argue that his presidency set a precedent for executive overreach which persisted through to the presidencies of Franklin Roosevelt, Lyndon Johnson, and Joseph Biden. After suffering a stroke that left him partially paralyzed, he refused to quit. He kept pushing for world peace, believing that big ideas take time to succeed. His efforts later inspired the United Nations, proving that persistence wins in the end.

Wilson's policies, while in office, arguably make him a president deserving of little or no admiration.

What Core Value Was Missing From His Legacy?

Respect: Woodrow Wilson had a vision for peace, but his actions at home told a different story. He supported segregation, looked down on the Constitution, and made decisions that left many Americans behind. His legacy reminds us that big ideas mean little without respect for all people.

Question: Can a leader still be great if they don't treat everyone with respect? Why is it important to pay attention to both someone's words and their actions?

Pimento Cheese Spread
A Nostalgic Classic

Just like American Innovation

Pimento Cheese Spread isn't just a Southern staple—it's a creamy, tangy, and downright addictive dish that represents comfort, tradition, and togetherness. Whether served at a Fourth of July picnic, a game-day gathering, this spread is as American as it gets!

James Monroe
"I shaped a doctrine—now shape your bite!"

Servings: 10–12

Ingredients:

- 2 cups sharp cheddar cheese, shredded
- 1 cup white cheddar cheese, shredded
- ½ cup cream cheese, softened
- ½ cup mayonnaise
- 1 jar (4 oz) pimentos, drained and finely chopped
- ½ teaspoon garlic powder
- ½ teaspoon onion powder
- ¼ teaspoon cayenne pepper (optional for heat)
- ½ teaspoon smoked paprika
- ½ teaspoon Dijon mustard
- 1 teaspoon Worcestershire sauce
- ¼ teaspoon salt (or to taste)
- ¼ teaspoon black pepper
- 1 tablespoon pickle juice (optional for tang)

Instructions to Bite Back Better!

- In a large mixing bowl, combine cream cheese, mayonnaise, Dijon mustard, and Worcestershire sauce. Mix until smooth.
- Stir in shredded cheeses, pimentos, garlic powder, onion powder, smoked paprika, cayenne, salt, and black pepper.
- Add pickle juice (if using) and mix until creamy and well combined.
- Chill for at least 30 minutes to let the flavors meld together.
- Serve with crackers, toasted baguette slices, or fresh veggies.

Fun Fact:

Pimento cheese was originally a delicacy in the early 1900s before becoming a Southern icon. It was even included in military rations during World War II.

Thematic Tie-In:

Much like America itself, pimento cheese is a fusion of flavors—bold, adaptable, and built on strong, simple ingredients that come together to create something greater.

Perfect Serving Occasions:

- Fourth of July BBQs 🍔
- Tailgates and Game Days 🏈
- Picnics and Family Gatherings 🧺 🥖
- Holiday Party Appetizers 🎊 🎇
- Anytime Snacking! 🥪

Drink Pairing:

- Classic Choice: Sweet tea—a true Southern match!
- Refreshing: Lemonade or sparkling water to balance the richness.
- For adults: A light beer or a crisp white wine like Sauvignon Blanc.

Ingredient Substitution Options:

- Lighter Option? Swap mayo for Greek yogurt or light sour cream.
- Dairy-Free? Use vegan mayo and dairy-free cheese.
- Spicier? Add hot sauce or diced jalapeños for extra kick.

DIY Presentation & Decorating Ideas:

- Star-Spangled Spread: Arrange in a star shape on a platter with red (pimentos), white (cheese), and blue (blue corn chips).
- Mason Jar Mini Servings: Perfect for picnics and parties!
- Cheese Board Extravaganza: Serve with nuts, grapes, and sliced meats for a patriotic charcuterie feel.

Ingredient Storytelling:

The pimento pepper originated in Spain and made its way to the U.S., where it found its home in Southern kitchens. Over the decades, it has become a beloved, nostalgic classic—just like American innovation itself!

James Monroe's Legacy:

In 1823, James Monroe faced a challenge—European powers were threatening to take over newly independent nations in the Americas. Many leaders might have backed down, afraid of upsetting powerful countries. But Monroe? He took a stand.

With the Monroe Doctrine, he sent a clear message: The Americas are not open for colonization—any attempt will be seen as a threat to the United States. At the time, America wasn't a global power yet, but Monroe believed in standing up for what was right, even against stronger opponents. And history proved him right—his doctrine shaped U.S. foreign policy for generations.

So, what does this mean for you? When faced with a challenge, don't let fear stop you. *Stand up for yourself,* your friends, or what you believe in—even when the odds seem stacked against you. You have the ability to be like Monroe, so don't wait.

Little known fact: Like two presidents before him, Jefferson and Adams, James Monroe died on July 4.

What Core Value Shaped His Legacy?

Service: James Monroe spent most of his life working for the country—as a soldier, diplomat, senator, and president. He focused on keeping the nation strong and united. The Monroe Doctrine helped protect U.S. interests, showing that long-term service can shape the future in big ways.

Question: What does it mean to serve something bigger than yourself? How can helping others today shape what comes tomorrow?

Tzatziki with Pita Bread
A Fusion for Great Taste

Yogurt-Based

Tzatziki is a refreshing, creamy, and tangy yogurt-based dip that has been a staple of Mediterranean cuisine for centuries. Whether enjoyed as a dip, a spread, or a topping, its garlic-infused, herb-packed, and cucumber-laced goodness makes it a perfect pairing for warm, fluffy pita bread.

Richard Nixon
"I opened China, but I should've opened more Tzatziki and Pita!"

Servings: **8–10** | **Prep Time:** 10 min | Chill Time: 30 min | **Cook Time:** 8–10 min

Tzatziki Sauce:

- 2 cups Greek yogurt (full-fat for best texture)
- 1 medium cucumber, grated and drained
- 2 cloves garlic, minced
- 1 tablespoon fresh lemon juice
- 1 tablespoon extra virgin olive oil
- 1 tablespoon fresh dill, finely chopped (or 1 teaspoon dried dill)
- ½ teaspoon salt (or to taste)
- ¼ teaspoon black pepper
- ½ teaspoon white vinegar (optional for extra tang)

For the Pita Bread:

- 4–6 pieces pita bread, cut into triangles
- 1 tablespoon olive oil
- ½ teaspoon garlic powder (optional for extra flavor)
- ½ teaspoon dried oregano (optional)
- Salt to taste

Instructions to Bite Back Better!

Make the Tzatziki Sauce:

- Prepare the cucumber: Grate the cucumber, then place it in a clean towel and squeeze out as much liquid as possible. This prevents the tzatziki from becoming watery.
- In a medium bowl, combine Greek yogurt, grated cucumber, minced garlic, lemon juice, olive oil, dill, salt, pepper, and vinegar. Stir well.
- Chill for at least 30 minutes to allow flavors to meld.

Prepare the Pita Bread:

- Preheat oven to 375°F (190°C).
- Arrange pita triangles on a baking sheet. Brush lightly with olive oil and sprinkle with garlic powder, oregano, and salt.
- Bake for 8–10 minutes or until lightly crispy and golden.
- Serve warm pita bread alongside the chilled tzatziki for the perfect Mediterranean dip experience!

Fun Fact:

Tzatziki dates back to ancient Greece, where a similar yogurt-based dip was enjoyed by warriors and athletes for its cooling and nourishing qualities!

Thematic Tie-In:

Like America's melting pot of cultures, tzatziki is a fusion of simple, bold ingredients coming together to create something greater. Just like great leadership and teamwork, it's all about balance!

Perfect Serving Occasions:

- Summer BBQs and picnics
- Game nights and appetizers
- Healthy snack or side dish
- Mediterranean-themed dinners
- Refreshing post-workout snack

Drink Pairing:

- Refreshing Choice: Lemon-infused water
- Classic Pairing: Iced mint tea
- For adults: A crisp white wine or light lager beer pairs beautifully!

Ingredient Substitution Options:

- Dairy-Free? Use coconut yogurt or dairy-free Greek-style yogurt.
- More Flavor? Add finely chopped mint or parsley for an herbaceous twist!
- Extra Creamy? Stir in 1 tablespoon sour cream for a richer texture.

DIY Presentation & Decorating Ideas:

- Garnish with a drizzle of olive oil and a sprig of dill for a restaurant-style look.
- Serve in small mason jars for a grab-and-go party snack.
- Pair with a platter of veggies, olives, and feta cheese for a Mediterranean feast.

Ingredient Storytelling:

Greek yogurt has been a staple of Mediterranean diets for thousands of years, prized for its high protein, probiotic benefits, and creamy texture. Combined with cooling cucumber and zesty garlic, tzatziki represents balance and tradition—a reminder that sometimes, the simplest ingredients make the most powerful impact.

Richard Nixon's Legacy:

Richard Nixon's legacy is complex, but one thing stands out: his ability to rise after failure. He lost the 1960 presidential race, was told his political career was over, yet he refused to quit. In 1968, he ran again and won, proving that *setbacks don't define you*—your persistence does.

As president, he opened relations with China, changing global diplomacy forever. He also created the EPA, protecting America's environment for future generations.

Yes, Nixon made mistakes, but his resilience and leadership prove a key lesson: failure isn't the end—if you learn, grow, and keep going, you can succeed.

What Core Value Was Missing From His Legacy?

Integrity: Richard Nixon achieved major successes, like opening relations with China and ending the Vietnam War. But the Watergate scandal—and his attempts to cover it up—broke the public's trust. His story shows how a lack of integrity can undo even the biggest accomplishments.

Question: Why is it important to stay honest, even when you're afraid of the consequences? What can happen when trust is broken?

Crab Cakes
Coastal Patriot Perfection

A Taste of the Shore
and a
Salute to American Ingenuity

Golden-crisp on the outside, tender and savory on the inside, these crab cakes bring the essence of coastal America to your plate.

Servings: 4 | **Prep Time:** 15 min | **Cook Time:** 10 min

James Madison
"I wrote the Constitution, now I'm perfecting crab cakes!"

Ingredients

- 1 pound lump crab meat *(the crown jewel of seafood)*
- 1/3 cup mayonnaise
- 1 large egg
- 1 teaspoon Dijon mustard *(adding a touch of sophistication)*
- 1 teaspoon Worcestershire sauce *(a classic flair)*
- 1 teaspoon Old Bay seasoning *(America's favorite crab seasoning)*
- 1/4 cup finely chopped parsley
- 1/2 cup panko breadcrumbs *(for that perfect crunch)*
- 2 tablespoons unsalted butter *(for pan-frying)*
- 1 lemon, cut into wedges *(for zesty patriotism)*

Instructions to Bite Back Better!

1. **Mix with Care:**
   In a large bowl, combine mayonnaise, egg, mustard, Worcestershire sauce, Old Bay seasoning, and parsley. Gently fold in the crab meat and breadcrumbs, taking care not to break up the crab too much.

2. **Form the Cakes:**
   Shape the mixture into 8 small cakes or 4 larger ones. Cover and refrigerate for 30 minutes to firm up.

3. **Pan-Fry to Golden Glory:**
   Heat butter in a skillet over medium heat. Fry the crab cakes for 4–5 minutes on each side until golden brown and cooked through.

4. **Serve with Pride:**
   Plate with lemon wedges for squeezing and a side of tartar or remoulade sauce.

Fun Fact: Crab cakes trace their roots to the Chesapeake Bay area, particularly Maryland, where crab fishing has been an economic and cultural cornerstone since the 1700s.

Thematic Tie-In: Crab cakes are a reminder of America's rich coastal heritage and the determination of its people to make something extraordinary out of simple, natural resources.

Serving Occasions:
- Summer Cookouts
- Family Gatherings
- Fourth of July Feasts

Serving Tips:
Garnish your plate with fresh herbs and serve alongside a patriotic slaw (red cabbage, white onion, and blue cheese dressing) for a festive presentation.

Inspiration Moment: Just like crafting the perfect crab cake, building confidence in our youth requires the right mix of encouragement and opportunity. Let this recipe inspire belief in their ability to create someone great!

James Madison's Legacy:
As the 4th President of the United States, he is often called the "Father of the Constitution" because he wrote it, the document that defines our government. His influence is everywhere, but you might notice it most on TV and in the news today.

Two of Madison's greatest achievements—the 1st and 2nd Amendments in the Bill of Rights—are constantly at the center of modern debates. From free speech and freedom of the press to the right to bear arms, these issues make Madison's impact more discussed than any other president.

Madison originally drafted the Bill of Rights to ensure the new government would protect individual freedoms. The 1st Amendment guarantees freedoms like speech, religion, and the press, while the 2nd Amendment protects the right to bear arms. Both remain some of the most talked-about parts of the Constitution.

Beyond the Bill of Rights, Madison's leadership in creating the U.S. Constitution and guiding the country through the War of 1812 cemented his legacy. While his presidency had challenges, his ideas shaped the nation. The fact that his amendments dominate conversations centuries later shows how deeply his vision for individual rights and freedoms influences us today.

At 5' 2" tall, James Madison was our shortest president.

Madison's legacy inspires young people today through his dedication to education, individual rights, and public service. How?

- **Education Matters:** Madison's rigorous studies show the power of learning in shaping society.
- **Defending Freedoms:** As the principal author of the Bill of Rights, he safeguarded speech, religion, and assembly.
- **Serving the Nation:** His leadership as a legislator, Secretary of State, and President highlights civic engagement.
- **Balanced Power:** He helped create checks and balances, ensuring government accountability.

Young people can learn from Madison's vision: valuing knowledge, protecting freedoms, and leading with integrity.

What Core Value Shaped His Legacy?

Humility: James Madison helped write the Constitution and the Bill of Rights, but he didn't brag or try to take all the credit. He preferred listening to others and worked behind the scenes. His story shows that humble people can still make a big difference, and that being humble often makes you more trustworthy: someone others count on to be honest, fair, and to do the right thing.

Question: Why do you think some people work hard without needing credit? How can humility help people trust and respect you more?

Smoked Salmon Crostini
Elegance in Every Bite

Combo of Simplicity and Balance

These bite-sized beauties combine rich, smoky salmon and creamy spread on crispy bread for a sophisticated yet approachable American classic.

Servings: 12 | **Prep Time:** 15 min | **Cook Time:** 10 min

Benjamin Harrison
"I stood for merit over favors—just like this dish stands on flavor!"

Ingredients:

- 1 baguette, sliced into 1/2-inch rounds
- 2 tablespoons olive oil *(for toasting the bread)*
- 8 ounces cream cheese, softened
- 1 tablespoon fresh dill, chopped *(plus extra for garnish)*
- 1 teaspoon lemon zest *(a bright pop of flavor)*
- 1 tablespoon lemon juice
- Salt and pepper, to taste
- 4 ounces smoked salmon, thinly sliced
- 1/4 cup capers *(optional, for briny goodness)*
- 1/4 cup red onion, finely sliced *(for a touch of sharp contrast)*

Instructions to Bite Back Better!

1. **Prepare the Crostini Base:**
   Preheat the oven to 400°F. Arrange the baguette slices on a baking sheet and brush lightly with olive oil. Bake for 8–10 minutes, until golden and crispy. Let cool slightly.

2. **Mix the Spread:**
   In a small bowl, combine softened cream cheese, lemon zest, lemon juice, dill, salt, and pepper. Stir until smooth and creamy.

3. **Assemble the Crostini:**
   Spread a layer of the cream cheese mixture onto each toasted baguette slice. Top with a delicate fold of smoked salmon.

4. Garnish and Serve:
Add a few capers, a sliver of red onion, and a sprinkle of fresh dill on top for color and flavor.

5. Plate with Style:
Arrange the crostini on a platter, garnished with lemon wedges for an elegant presentation.

Fun Fact: Smoked salmon, or *lox*, was popularized in the United States in the early 20th century by Eastern European immigrants. Today, it's a celebrated component of American brunch and party platters.

History: Smoked salmon has deep roots in preservation techniques used across Nordic and Native American cultures. Combined with crostini (Italian for "little crusts"), this dish highlights the beauty of global influences on American cuisine.

Serving Tip:

Serve these smoked salmon crostini as an elegant appetizer at brunches, garden parties, or patriotic gatherings. They pair beautifully with fresh greens or a light, citrusy salad.

Drink Pairing:

Pair with a crisp glass of **Prosecco** or a light, citrusy **sauvignon blanc** to complement the smokiness of the salmon. Non-alcoholic? A sparkling lemon spritzer or cucumber-infused water works perfectly.

Inspiration Moment: Smoked Salmon Crostini prove that elegance is found in simplicity and balance. By celebrating small, purposeful steps, we can teach young people to combine their strengths into something beautiful—just like these little toasts that pack a big impression.

Benjamin Harrison's Legacy:
Benjamin Harrison believed that leadership isn't given, it's earned through action. Long before becoming president, he showed that standing up for what's right, even when it's tough, is what makes a real difference.

During the Civil War, Harrison could have stayed safe as a politician, but instead, he volunteered for the Union Army and led his soldiers into battle. He didn't wait for someone else to act; he took responsibility, led from the front, and earned their respect.

So what does this mean for you? You don't have to be in a war to step up and lead. Speak up when something's unfair. Take charge in your school or community. Whether it's organizing a fundraiser, standing up for a friend, or helping those in need—leaders act, no matter the risk.

Harrison proved that you *don't wait for change; instead, you make it.* So what will you do today?

What Core Value Shaped His Legacy?
Accountability: Benjamin Harrison believed leaders should take responsibility for their actions. He supported fair voting rights and protected natural lands, even when those choices weren't popular. His story shows that being honest about your actions—even the hard ones—can earn lasting respect.
Question: Why do people respect someone who takes responsibility, even when it's hard for them to do?

Oysters Rockefeller
A Real Sea-Change

Decadent Bite of American Luxury

Rich, savory, and a little fancy, these baked oysters bring sophistication to any celebration while honoring a timeless American classic.

Servings: 12 oysters (4–6 servings) | **Prep Time:** 20 min | **Cook Time:** 15 min

Franklin D. Roosevelt
"I led the nation to victory in WWII—now savor the success!"

Ingredients:

- 12 fresh oysters, shucked, on the half shell
- 4 tablespoons unsalted butter *(for sautéing)*
- 2 cloves garlic, minced
- 2 cups fresh spinach, finely chopped
- 1/4 cup parsley, finely chopped
- 2 tablespoons Pernod (or white wine) *(adds depth of flavor)*
- 1/2 cup breadcrumbs *(panko for extra crispiness)*
- 1/2 cup Parmesan cheese, grated
- 1 tablespoon lemon juice *(brightens the richness)*
- 1 teaspoon hot sauce *(optional, for a patriotic kick)*
- Salt and black pepper, to taste
- Rock salt or coarse salt *(for baking stability)*
- Lemon wedges, for serving

Instructions to Bite Back Better*!*

1. **Preheat and Prepare:**
   Preheat your oven to 450°F. Spread a layer of rock salt on a baking sheet to keep the oysters stable during baking.

2. **Make the Topping:**
   In a skillet over medium heat, melt butter. Sauté garlic until fragrant (1 minute). Add spinach, parsley, and Pernod (or wine) and cook until the greens wilt. Stir in breadcrumbs, Parmesan cheese, lemon juice, and hot sauce. Season with salt and pepper.

3. **Top the Oysters:**
   Place the shucked oysters on the prepared baking sheet. Spoon 1–2 tablespoons of the spinach mixture onto each oyster, ensuring an even coating.

4. Bake to Perfection:
Bake for 10–12 minutes, or until the topping is golden brown and bubbly.

5. Serve with Flair:
Serve hot with lemon wedges on the side for a final burst of brightness.

Fun Fact: Oysters Rockefeller was invented in 1899 at Antoine's Restaurant in New Orleans. Named for John D. Rockefeller—then the richest man in America—this dish's decadent richness was meant to reflect his wealth.

History: This iconic dish is a symbol of American culinary ingenuity. Combining French influence with New Orleans flavors, it showcases how creativity and cultural blending have shaped the nation's food traditions.

Serving Tip:

Serve oysters on a bed of rock salt or crushed ice for a stunning presentation. Garnish with lemon wedges and a sprinkle of fresh parsley for extra flair.

Drink Pairing:

Pair these decadent oysters with a chilled glass of Champagne or a crisp Chablis (dry white wine) to complement the buttery richness. Non-alcoholic? Sparkling water with a splash of lemon or white grape juice works beautifully.

Inspiration for America's Youth: Oysters Rockefeller remind us that greatness often comes from simple ingredients elevated with care and creativity. Like this classic dish, young Americans can discover their potential, refining their talents to shine with brilliance and purpose.

Franklin D. Roosevelt's Legacy:
When Franklin D. Roosevelt became president in 1933, America was in crisis—jobs were gone, banks were failing, and people were losing hope. But instead of making excuses, Roosevelt took action and proved that real leaders step up when things get tough.

First, he launched the New Deal, creating millions of jobs through public works projects, proving that hard times demand bold solutions.

Then, when World War II threatened the world, Roosevelt led America to victory, showing that strength and determination can overcome any enemy.

And despite being unable to walk due to polio, he still led with confidence, proving that physical limits don't define your impact.

So what's the point? Don't wait for change; be the one to make it. Whether helping your school, pushing past struggles, or standing for what's right, you have *within you* the power to change your circumstances. So use your power!

What Core Value Shaped His Legacy?
Perseverance: Franklin D. Roosevelt led the country through the Great Depression and World War II. Even after losing the use of his legs, he never gave up. His steady leadership during hard times showed that perseverance means pushing forward—even when everything feels like it's falling apart.
Question: When have you had to keep going even though something felt too hard? What helped you stay strong instead of giving up?

Calamari Rings
A Crispy, Golden Celebration of Flavor

That's Italian!

These tender, crispy rings of calamari bring a taste of the sea to your table—perfect for sharing, celebrating, and savoring life's simple joys.

Servings: 4–6 | **Prep Time:** 15 min | **Cook Time:** 10 min

William McKinley
"I built prosperity—now savor a crispy taste of it!"

Ingredients:

- 1 pound squid rings *(cleaned and patted dry)*
- 1 cup all-purpose flour *(the golden coating foundation)*
- 1/2 cup cornstarch *(for extra crispiness)*
- 1 teaspoon garlic powder
- 1 teaspoon paprika *(a smoky hint of spice)*
- 1/2 teaspoon salt
- 1/2 teaspoon black pepper
- 2 eggs, beaten
- Vegetable oil, for frying
- 1 lemon, cut into wedges *(for serving)*

For the Dipping Sauce:

- 1/2 cup mayonnaise
- 2 tablespoons ketchup
- 1 teaspoon lemon juice
- 1/2 teaspoon hot sauce *(optional for a zesty kick)*

Instructions to Bite Back Better!

1. **Prepare the Squid:**
   Pat the squid rings dry with paper towels to ensure they fry up crispy.

2. **Make the Coating:**
   In a large bowl, combine flour, cornstarch, garlic powder, paprika, salt, and black pepper.

3. **Dip and Coat:**
   Dip each squid ring into the beaten eggs, then dredge in the flour mixture until fully coated. Shake off any excess flour.

4. **Fry to Perfection:**
   Heat about 2 inches of vegetable oil in a deep skillet or pot to 350°F. Fry the squid rings in batches for 2–3 minutes, until golden brown and crispy. Avoid overcrowding the pan.

5. Drain and Serve:

Remove the calamari with a slotted spoon and drain on paper towels. Serve hot with lemon wedges and the prepared dipping sauce.

6. Make the Sauce:

In a small bowl, whisk together mayonnaise, ketchup, lemon juice, and hot sauce until smooth.

Fun Fact: Calamari, which comes from the Italian word for squid, has been enjoyed for centuries in Mediterranean cuisines. In America, it became a popular appetizer in the 1970s and has since become a staple on menus across the country.

History: Calamari rings reflect the blending of Italian and American culinary traditions. Originally a beloved Mediterranean dish, it quickly became an all-American favorite at seafood restaurants, showcasing the beauty of cross-cultural influence.

Serving Tip:

Serve calamari on a platter garnished with fresh parsley and lemon wedges. Pair with marinara sauce for a classic twist or the zesty dipping sauce for a modern flair.

Drink Pairing:

Pair these crispy rings with a chilled glass of **Pinot Grigio** or a refreshing **pale ale** to balance the crunch and richness. Non-alcoholic option? Try a sparkling lemonade or citrus-infused iced tea for a bright, refreshing complement.

Inspiration Moment: Calamari rings remind us that even the simplest ingredients—when treated with care—can shine brightly. Just like these golden rings, young Americans can turn their small efforts into extraordinary achievements with the right mix of preparation and confidence. For example, Charlie Kirk started TPUSA at age 18 and turned it into a national movement at colleges.

William McKinley's Legacy:

When William McKinley became president, America was changing fast. One of his biggest challenges was the Spanish-American War in 1898. Instead of rushing into battle, McKinley tried diplomacy first, but when war became unavoidable, he led with confidence.

In just a few months, America won, and McKinley helped the nation emerge as a world power. Plus, he worked to help the people in the new territories, like Puerto Rico and the Philippines, while also strengthening the U.S. economy through fair trade policies.

So why does this matter to you? Because real leaders think before they act; that's not hard, is it? McKinley didn't jump into war recklessly, he weighed his options, stayed calm under pressure, and made the best decision.

As a young student, you'll face tough choices. Take McKinley's approach: think critically, stay steady, and lead with confidence. That's how you make a real impact.

William McKinley was a young soldier in the Civil War. After a long battle, his fellow soldiers were exhausted and hungry. McKinley volunteered to bring them food, riding through enemy fire to deliver hot coffee and rations.

This small act of bravery and kindness earned him the respect of his men. It wasn't about politics or power, it was about caring for others, even in danger. Which may be the reason the US Army adopted of the principle: "No soldier left behind."

McKinley's leadership wasn't loud, but it was steady and selfless, a reminder that true greatness comes from serving others first.

What Core Value Shaped His Legacy?

Kindness: William McKinley was known for treating others with respect and warmth, even in politics. He believed in leading with calm words instead of anger and cared deeply about doing what was best for the country. His kindness helped bring people together during a changing time in history.

Question: Why does being kind matter, even when you're in charge or under pressure? Can kindness make someone a stronger leader?

Lobster Roll

A New England Favorite from the Sea

A Luxury Delicacy Enjoyed Worldwide

Originating from New England, this dish is a symbol of American seafood excellence. Whether served Maine-style (cold with mayo) or Connecticut-style (warm with butter), the lobster roll is a celebration of simple ingredients done right.

John F. Kennedy
"I set new frontiers. Now set your table with a lobster roll!"

Servings: 4 | **Prep Time:** 15 min | **Chill Time:** 15 min | **Cook Time:** 5 min

Quick Tip: If using pre-cooked lobster meat, the recipe can be ready in as little as 15 minutes!

For the Lobster Filling (Maine-Style - Cold Version):

- 1 lb cooked lobster meat, chopped (claws and tail preferred)
- ¼ cup mayonnaise
- 1 tablespoon fresh lemon juice
- ½ teaspoon Dijon mustard
- ½ teaspoon Old Bay seasoning (optional)
- ¼ teaspoon garlic powder
- 1 tablespoon chopped fresh chives or parsley
- Salt and black pepper to taste

For the Lobster Filling (CT-Style - Warm Version):

- 1 lb cooked lobster meat, chopped
- 4 tablespoons melted butter
- ½ teaspoon lemon zest
- 1 tablespoon fresh lemon juice
- ½ teaspoon garlic powder
- Salt and black pepper to taste

For the Buns:

- 4 New England-style split-top hot dog buns
- 2 tablespoons butter, softened
- ½ teaspoon garlic powder (optional, for extra flavor)

Instructions to Bite Back Better!

Step 1: Prepare the Lobster Filling

For Maine-Style (Cold Lobster Roll):

- In a bowl, mix lobster meat, mayonnaise, lemon juice, Dijon mustard, Old Bay seasoning, garlic powder, chives, salt, and black pepper.

- Stir well and chill for at least 15 minutes to let the flavors blend.

For Connecticut-Style (Warm Lobster Roll):
- Melt butter in a small pan, then stir in lemon zest, lemon juice, garlic powder, salt, and pepper.
- Add lobster meat and cook for 2-3 minutes, just until warmed through.

Step 2: Toast the Buns
- Heat a skillet or griddle over medium heat.
- Spread butter on the outer sides of the split-top buns and sprinkle lightly with garlic powder (if using).
- Toast buns for 1-2 minutes per side until golden brown and crispy.

Step 3: Assemble the Lobster Rolls
- Fill each toasted bun generously with either the chilled lobster salad (Maine-style) or the buttery lobster mixture (Connecticut-style).
- Garnish with extra chives or a squeeze of fresh lemon.
- Serve immediately with chips, fries, or coleslaw for the ultimate experience!

Fun Fact:
Lobster rolls became popular in Maine in the 1920s, but lobster itself was once considered "poor man's food" and fed to prisoners and servants! Today, it's a luxury delicacy enjoyed worldwide.

Thematic Tie-In:
Just like America, the lobster roll is about balance—whether warm or cold, buttery or creamy, its flavors reflect the rich diversity and boldness of American cuisine.

Perfect Serving Occasions:
- Fourth of July Cookouts
- Beach Picnics and Summer BBQs
- Game Day and Tailgates
- Family Dinners and Seafood Feasts
- Anytime You Want a Taste of the Coast!

Drink Pairing:
- Classic Choice: Lemonade or iced tea for a refreshing balance.
- For a New England Vibe: Cold craft beer pairs beautifully.
- For a Fancier Feel: Chilled white wine (Chardonnay or Sauvignon Blanc)

Ingredient Substitution Options:
- No Fresh Lobster? Use high-quality canned or frozen lobster meat.
- Dairy-Free? Swap butter for olive oil in the Connecticut-style version.
- Lighter Option? Use Greek yogurt instead of mayo for a tangier, healthier twist.

DIY Presentation & Decorating Ideas:
- Garnish with lemon wedges and fresh herbs for a vibrant, restaurant-style look.
- Serve in mini rolls for party-sized bites—perfect for appetizers!
- Pair with a side of coleslaw and pickles for a complete New England meal.

Ingredient Storytelling:
Lobster rolls are a symbol of American ingenuity—turning what was once overlooked into a beloved classic. Just like in life, sometimes the best things come from humble beginnings and bold choices.

Closing Thought for America's Youth:
Whether in food or life, success is about finding the right balance—between boldness and simplicity, tradition and innovation. Like the lobster roll, your path may take twists and turns, but with the right ingredients, you can create something unforgettable.

John Kennedy's Legacy:
He inspired America to dream big and take action. He challenged the nation to land on the moon, proving that impossible goals can be achieved *with vision and effort*. He also fought for civil rights, pushing for fairness and equality. Despite obstacles, he believed in courage, service, and leadership. His most inspiring message to all of us:

> **"Ask not what your country can do for you; ask what you can do for your country."**

Have you ever done something to help others without being asked? Why do you think serving others can make a difference in the world? In *your* world?

Tuna Tartare
A Blend of Cultures

French, Japanese, and American

John Tyler
"Annexing Texas was big! So is the flavor in this dish!"

Tuna Tartare is a light, refreshing, and sophisticated dish that blends the buttery richness of raw tuna with zesty citrus, creamy avocado, and bold seasonings. Originally inspired by French and Japanese cuisine, this dish has become a staple in modern American dining—a perfect balance of simplicity and elegance.

Servings: 4 | **Prep Time**: 15 min (chopping and mixing) | **Chill Time** (optional): 15 min (for deeper flavor) | **Cook Time:** not required | **Total Time:** 15–30 min (depending on chilling time)

For the Tuna Tartare:

- 1 lb sushi-grade tuna, finely diced
- 1 small avocado, finely diced
- 2 tablespoons soy sauce
- 1 tablespoon sesame oil
- 1 tablespoon fresh lime juice (or lemon juice)
- 1 teaspoon Dijon mustard
- ½ teaspoon grated ginger
- ½ teaspoon garlic, minced
- 1 teaspoon honey or agave syrup (optional)
- 1 small shallot, finely minced
- 1 tablespoon chopped fresh cilantro or chives
- ½ teaspoon red pepper flakes (optional for heat)
- Salt & black pepper to taste

For Garnish & Serving:

- 1 tablespoon black or white sesame seeds
- 1 teaspoon sriracha or chili oil (for spice)
- 4 teaspoons crème fraîche or wasabi mayo (optional)
- Microgreens or additional chives for topping
- Crispy wonton chips, crackers, or cucumber slices for serving

Prep Time & Cook Time:

- Prep Time: 15 minutes (chopping and mixing)
- Chill Time (optional): 15 minutes (for deeper flavor)
- Cook Time: 0 minutes (no cooking required!)
- Total Time: 15–30 minutes (depending on chilling time)

Instructions to Bite Back Better*!*

Step 1: Prepare the Tuna Tartare

- Dice the tuna into small, even cubes and place in a mixing bowl.
- Add soy sauce, sesame oil, lime juice, Dijon mustard, grated ginger, minced garlic, honey, shallot, cilantro (or chives), red pepper flakes, salt, and black pepper.
- Gently stir to combine without mashing the tuna.
- Fold in the diced avocado last to keep it from getting mushy.

Step 2: Chill & Assemble

- For best flavor, let the mixture chill for 15 minutes in the fridge.
- To serve, use a ring mold (or gently shape by hand) to create neat rounds of tartare on plates.
- Sprinkle with sesame seeds and microgreens.
- Drizzle with sriracha or chili oil for extra heat.
- Top with a dollop of crème fraîche or wasabi mayo for a creamy touch.
- Serve with crispy wonton chips, crackers, or cucumber slices for dipping!

Fun Fact:

Tartare dishes were originally inspired by steak tartare in France, but chefs later adapted the technique to seafood, creating a luxurious yet simple dish loved worldwide!

Thematic Tie-In:

Just like American innovation, Tuna Tartare is a blend of cultures—bringing together French technique, Japanese influence, and fresh American seafood. A perfect example of how great things happen when we mix bold ideas!

Perfect Serving Occasions:

- Elegant Dinner Parties
- Date Nights & Special Occasions
- Light & Healthy Appetizers
- Summertime Refreshments
- Gourmet Game Day Snacks

Drink Pairing:

- Crisp White Wine (Sauvignon Blanc or Riesling)
- Dry Sparkling Wine or Champagne
- Chilled Sake or Light Beer
- Refreshing Citrus-Infused Sparkling Water

Ingredient Substitution Options:

- No Tuna? Use sushi-grade salmon for a delicious twist!
- Soy-Free? Substitute coconut aminos for soy sauce.
- Spicier? Add extra sriracha or a pinch of wasabi.
- Lighter Option? Swap avocado for finely diced cucumber.

DIY Presentation & Decorating Ideas:

- Serve in mini shot glasses or on cucumber slices for a fancy party appetizer.
- Garnish with edible flowers or microgreens for a restaurant-style look.
- Layer tartare on crispy wonton chips for bite-sized tuna tartare nachos!

John Tyler's Legacy for Today's Youth:

As the 10th U.S. president (1841–1845), he left a legacy of resilience, bold decision-making, and commitment to principle—qualities that can inspire today's youth. When President William Henry Harrison died, Tyler became the first vice president to assume the presidency, setting a lasting precedent for presidential succession. Plus, he fathered 15 children (cable TV wasn't available back then). Though faced with opposition, he stood firm in his beliefs, even risking political isolation. His advocacy for states' rights and expansion led to the annexation of Texas, shaping America's future. Tyler's determination, willingness to defy expectations, and courage in leadership teach young people the importance of perseverance, standing by their convictions, and making tough decisions even when unpopular—valuable character traits for future leaders and "interrupters."

What Core Value Shaped His Legacy?

Self-Reliance: John Tyler became president suddenly after the death of William Henry Harrison, and many people doubted him. But he stood his ground, made decisions on his own, and didn't let others control him. His story shows the power of believing in yourself when no one else does.

Question: Have you ever had to prove yourself when others didn't believe in you? What helped you stay confident and keep going?

Shrimp Cocktail
Big Bites, Big Flavor

Impress the Guests

Thomas Jefferson
"I founded a nation. Now I found the perfect appetizer."

Chilled, elegant, and full of zesty flavor, shrimp cocktail is the timeless appetizer that never goes out of style. With perfectly poached shrimp and a bold, tangy dipping sauce, it's fresh, light, and sure to impress guests at any gathering.

Servings: 4-6 | **Prep Time:** 15 minutes | **Cook Time:** 3–4 min | **Chill Time:** 15–20 min

For the Shrimp

- 1 lb large shrimp (16/20 count), peeled and deveined, tails on
- 1 lemon, halved
- 1 teaspoon salt
- 1 teaspoon black peppercorns
- 2 garlic cloves, smashed
- 2–3 sprigs fresh parsley (optional)
- 4 cups water

For the Cocktail Sauce

- ½ cup ketchup
- 2 tablespoons prepared horseradish (more for extra kick)
- 1 tablespoon fresh lemon juice
- 1 teaspoon Worcestershire sauce
- ½ teaspoon hot sauce (optional)
- Salt and pepper, to taste

Instructions to Bite Back Better!

Step 1: Make the Cocktail Sauce

- In a small bowl, mix ketchup, horseradish, lemon juice, Worcestershire, and hot sauce.
- Season with salt and pepper to taste.
- Chill in the fridge until ready to serve.

Step 2: Poach the Shrimp

- In a medium saucepan, bring water, lemon halves, salt, peppercorns, garlic, and parsley to a boil.
- Reduce to a simmer, then add the shrimp.
- Cook for 2–3 minutes, just until pink and opaque.
- Immediately transfer shrimp to an ice bath to stop cooking. Chill for at least 15 minutes.

Step 3: Serve & Enjoy

- Arrange shrimp around a cocktail glass or platter, with a bowl of the chilled sauce in the center.
- Garnish with lemon wedges and fresh herbs if desired.

Perfect Serving Suggestions

- Serve as a starter for formal dinners or holiday meals.
- Add to a seafood platter with oysters and crab legs.
- Pair with a crisp salad or chilled pasta for a light lunch.

Drink Pairing

- **Kids:** Sparkling water with lemon or cucumber
- **Adults:** Dry white wine, prosecco, or a classic martini

Fun Fact

Shrimp cocktail became a dinner party staple in the 1960s, but its roots go back to early 20th-century seafood houses, where it was considered a luxury!

Thematic Tie-In: Elegant, Simple, and Classic

Like a great leader, shrimp cocktail proves that refinement and strength can come from simplicity and balance.

Ingredient Substitution Options

- **No Horseradish?** Use Dijon mustard or a dab of wasabi for a similar kick.
- **No Worcestershire?** Try soy sauce or tamari for umami flavor.
- **Pre-cooked Shrimp?** Just thaw, chill, and serve—no poaching needed.

DIY Presentation & Decorating Ideas

- Serve in martini glasses with shrimp hanging over the rim.
- Use a patriotic tray with small American flags as toothpicks.
- Add crushed ice under the shrimp for extra chill and flair.

How Jefferson Helps With Character Development:
His legacy offers several powerful lessons for character development, especially in the areas of curiosity, responsibility, and civic virtue. While Jefferson was a complex and imperfect figure, the values he championed for a new nation still offer meaningful guidance for today's youth.

1. Intellectual Curiosity and Lifelong Learning
Jefferson was a passionate learner, inventor, writer, and thinker. He read voraciously, studied science, architecture, and languages, and founded the University of Virginia. His example teaches youth that developing character includes feeding the mind—being curious, asking questions, and pursuing knowledge beyond the classroom.

2. Commitment to Principles
As the principal author of the Declaration of Independence, Jefferson gave voice to the idea that all people are born with inherent rights. While he struggled to fully live out those ideals, his words still teach teens that standing for freedom, equality, and justice matters, and that great character includes fighting for what's right, even when it's hard.

3. Civic Responsibility
Jefferson believed that a strong nation required informed, active citizens. He inspires youth to care about their communities, engage in meaningful dialogue, and take their role in democracy seriously.

4. Vision and Innovation
Jefferson thought far ahead—about education, government, and growth. He teaches youth to think big, create, and contribute to a better future with integrity and imagination.

Check out his legacy narrative on page 82.

Coconut Shrimp
Sweet and Crunchy

An Island And Seafood Tradition

Coconut shrimp brings the perfect tropical crunch—crispy on the outside, juicy on the inside, and bursting with sweet and savory flavor. Whether you're hosting a party or craving a restaurant-style snack at home, this crowd-pleaser is easy to make and hard to resist.

Calvin Coolidge
"Low talker, high taste: Coolidge approved."

Servings: 4 (about 16 shrimp)
Time: 20 min | **Cook Time:** 5–6 min

For the Shrimp

- 1 lb large shrimp (16/20 count), peeled and deveined, tails on
- ½ cup all-purpose flour
- ½ teaspoon salt
- ½ teaspoon garlic powder
- ¼ teaspoon black pepper
- 2 large eggs
- ¾ cup panko breadcrumbs
- ¾ cup sweetened shredded coconut
- Vegetable oil for frying

For the Dipping Sauce (Optional but Delicious)

- ¼ cup orange marmalade
- 1 tablespoon Dijon mustard
- 1 teaspoon sriracha or hot sauce (optional, for a kick)
- 1 teaspoon lime juice

Instructions to Bite Back Better*!*

Step 1: Prepare the Dipping Sauce

- Mix orange marmalade, Dijon mustard, sriracha, and lime juice in a small bowl.
- Chill until ready to serve.

Step 2: Set Up the Breading Station

- In one shallow bowl, mix flour, salt, garlic powder, and pepper.
- In a second bowl, beat the eggs.
- In a third bowl, combine panko breadcrumbs and shredded coconut.

Step 3: Bread the Shrimp

- Dredge each shrimp in the flour mixture, then dip into the egg, then press into the coconut-panko mixture, coating well.
- Place on a tray and repeat with remaining shrimp.

Step 4: Fry the Shrimp

- Heat 2–3 inches of oil in a deep skillet or pot to 350°F (175°C).
- Fry shrimp in batches for 2–3 minutes per side, or until golden brown and cooked through.
- Transfer to a paper towel-lined plate to drain.

Tip: Want to bake or air fry instead? See **Ingredient Substitutions Options** below!

Perfect Serving Suggestions

- Serve with dipping sauce, pineapple salsa, or coleslaw.
- Pair with coconut rice, tropical salad, or grilled pineapple.
- Great as an appetizer or light dinner with a fruity cocktail.

Drink Pairing

- **Kids:** Pineapple juice or coconut water
- **Adults:** A chilled piña colada, white wine spritzer, or citrus mojito

Fun Fact

Though often associated with tropical cuisine, coconut shrimp became popular in the 1980s as fusion foods brought together island ingredients and American seafood traditions.

Thematic Tie-In: Bold, Bright, and Flavorful

Like confident leaders, coconut shrimp stands out—bold in flavor, unique in texture, and always leaves a lasting impression.

Ingredient Substitution Options

- **Baked Version:** Bake at 425°F (220°C) on a greased baking sheet for 15–18 minutes, flipping halfway through.
- **Air Fryer:** Air fry at 400°F (200°C) for 10–12 minutes, shaking halfway through.
- **Gluten-Free:** Use GF flour and breadcrumbs.
- **Unsweetened Coconut:** Works well for a more savory option.

DIY Presentation & Decorating Ideas
- Serve in a pineapple half for a tropical presentation.
- Use mini skewers for party-style finger food.
- Line your platter with banana leaves or colorful paper for festive flair.

How Coolidge Inspires Character Development:
Often remembered as "Silent Cal," he offers a quiet but powerful example for youth character development. In a world filled with noise and pressure to constantly perform, Coolidge's legacy reminds young people that character isn't about volume—*it's about values. Check out* page 34 for his legacy narrative.

1. Integrity and Honesty
Coolidge was known for his strong moral compass. He believed that public service was a sacred trust and lived by the principle that doing the right thing quietly was better than boasting loudly. Teens can learn that trustworthiness and integrity are the foundation of strong character and leadership.

2. Self-Discipline and Restraint
Coolidge practiced personal discipline and believed in doing more by saying less. In a culture of oversharing, instant reactions, and rash judgments, his restraint teaches youth the power of thinking before speaking—and the value of calm, measured responses.

3. Respect for Responsibility
Coolidge took his presidential duties seriously, never using power recklessly. This models for teens the importance of taking ownership of their actions and being responsible with what they're given—whether it's a team, a task, or a talent.

4. Humility and Service
He didn't seek attention, yet served with dignity. Coolidge shows young people that you don't need to be loud to be great. Serve humbly, live honestly, and lead with quiet strength.

Why is doing your job well, even when no one's watching, an important kind of responsibility? Can quiet actions make a big impact?

Clam Chowder Shooters
New England Version

Creamy and Comforting

Rich, creamy, and perfectly portioned, Clam Chowder Shooters deliver a taste of coastal comfort in every sip-sized serving. Ideal for parties or elegant starters, this appetizer brings big flavor in a small glass.

Servings: 12 | **Time:** 15 min | **Cook Time:** 30 min

Theodore Roosevelt
"These shooters? National treasures!"

For the Chowder
- 4 slices bacon, chopped
- 2 tablespoons unsalted butter
- ½ yellow onion, finely diced
- 1 celery stalk, finely diced
- 2 cloves garlic, minced
- 2 tablespoons all-purpose flour
- 2 cups bottled clam juice
- 1 cup heavy cream
- 1 cup whole milk
- 1 medium russet potato, peeled and diced small
- 1 (6.5 oz) can chopped clams, drained (reserve the juice)
- ½ teaspoon dried thyme
- Salt and freshly ground black pepper, to taste
- 1 tablespoon chopped fresh parsley (for garnish)

Optional Toppings
- Crumbled bacon
- Oyster crackers
- Mini sourdough toasts
- Fresh herbs

Instructions to Bite Back Better!

Step 1: Cook the Bacon
- In a large pot over medium heat, cook the chopped bacon until crispy.
- Remove and set aside on a paper towel. Leave about 1 tablespoon of fat in the pot.

Step 2: Sauté the Base
- Add butter, then sauté the onion, celery, and garlic until soft and translucent (3–4 minutes).
- Stir in flour to create a roux. Cook for 1 minute, stirring constantly.

Step 3: Build the Broth

- Slowly whisk in clam juice and reserved clam liquid to avoid lumps.
- Stir in milk, cream, thyme, and diced potatoes. Simmer for 15–18 minutes, or until potatoes are tender.

Step 4: Add Clams & Bacon

- Stir in the chopped clams and half the cooked bacon. Simmer for another 3–5 minutes.
- Season with salt and pepper to taste.

Step 5: Serve in Shooters

- Carefully ladle chowder into small shooter glasses.
- Garnish with bacon bits, oyster crackers, or chopped parsley. Serve warm with mini spoons.

Perfect Serving Suggestions

- Pair with a seafood platter or mini crab cakes.
- Serve with mini sourdough bowls or crusty bread rounds.
- Great addition to holiday hors d'oeuvres or cocktail parties.

Drink Pairing

- Kids: Sparkling apple cider or lemonade
- Adults: Dry white wine (like Chardonnay), or a New England-style IPA

Fun Fact

Clam chowder has regional variations, but the New England version—creamy and comforting—is the most iconic. It's been warming hearts since the 1700s.

Thematic Tie-In: Small But Mighty

Just like great leadership, chowder shooters deliver richness and impact in compact form—proof that big things often come in small packages.

Substitution Options

- Dairy-Free: Use oat milk and coconut cream (won't be as rich, but still satisfying).
- Meat-Free: Skip the bacon and use smoked paprika for depth.
- Gluten-Free: Replace flour with cornstarch or a GF flour blend.

Presentation & Decor Ideas

- Serve on a mini tray with sea shells for coastal flair.
- Use red, white, and blue shooters for patriotic themes.
- Tie mini American flags around the spoons for festive fun.

How Roosevelt Inspires Character Development:

Teddy Roosevelt's legacy is a goldmine for youth character development. He didn't just talk about values—he lived them boldly, and his life story gives young people real, actionable traits to build a stronger, more resilient character.

1. Grit and Personal Growth

As a sickly child, Roosevelt could've lived a limited life—but instead, he chose to toughen up, both physically and mentally. This relentless self-improvement teaches teens that they are not stuck with their starting point. They can grow stronger through effort, not excuses.

2. The "Strenuous Life" Mindset

Roosevelt preached the importance of embracing hard work, challenge, and discomfort. His philosophy teaches young people that character is built when they push themselves, get uncomfortable, and don't back down from life's tough moments.

3. Courage to Do What's Right

Whether taking on corrupt politicians or big corporations, Roosevelt stood his ground. He shows youth that character includes moral courage—doing the right thing, even when it's unpopular.

4. Love of Learning and Nature

Roosevelt was both a deep reader and a passionate conservationist. He teaches teens to stay curious, stay active, and stay connected to something bigger than themselves.

5. Action-Oriented Leadership

Roosevelt didn't wait—he charged forward. His legacy inspires youth to take initiative, lead boldly, and live with purpose.

Check out Roosevelt's legacy narrative on page 70.

Spring Rolls
Freshness with Crunch

Blending Flavors and Textures

Crisp, refreshing, and bursting with flavor, Spring Rolls are a delightful blend of crunchy vegetables, aromatic herbs, and either shrimp, chicken, or tofu—all wrapped in delicate rice paper or a crispy fried shell. Originating from Southeast Asia, these versatile rolls offer a perfect combination of texture, freshness, and dipping sauce magic.

Zackary Taylor
"I'm rough and ready... to enjoy these delicious spring rolls!

Servings: 4 | **Prep Time:** 20 min (chopping & rolling) | **Cook Time:** 5 min (fried option)

For the Spring Rolls (Choose Fresh or Fried):
- 8 rice paper wrappers (for fresh rolls) or egg roll wrappers (for fried rolls)
- 1 cup cooked shrimp, shredded chicken, or tofu strips
- 1 cup shredded carrots
- 1 cup shredded purple cabbage
- 1 small cucumber, julienned
- ½ cup fresh mint leaves
- ½ cup fresh cilantro leaves
- ½ cup fresh basil leaves
- 1 avocado, thinly sliced (optional)
- 4 ounces rice vermicelli noodles, cooked (optional for fresh rolls)
- 1 egg, whisked (for sealing fried rolls)

For the Dipping Sauce:
- ¼ cup hoisin sauce
- 2 tablespoons peanut butter
- 1 tablespoon soy sauce
- 1 teaspoon rice vinegar
- 1 teaspoon sesame oil
- 1 teaspoon honey or maple syrup
- 1 clove garlic, minced
- 1 tablespoon crushed peanuts for garnish

Instructions to Bite Back Better!

Step 1: Prep the Filling
- Slice all vegetables into thin strips for easy rolling.
- If making fresh rolls, soak rice paper wrappers in warm water for 10 seconds until pliable.
- If making fried rolls, keep egg roll wrappers dry and ready to roll.

Step 2: Assemble the Rolls

- **For Fresh Rolls:** Lay a rice paper wrapper flat. Layer protein, vegetables, herbs, and noodles in the center. Fold the sides in, then roll tightly.
- **For Fried Rolls:** Place filling in an egg roll wrapper, fold the sides, roll tightly, and seal the edge with whisked egg.

Step 3: Fry (Optional)

- Heat oil in a pan over medium heat. Fry rolls for 2–3 minutes per side until golden brown. Drain on paper towels.

Step 4: Make the Sauce & Serve

- Whisk all dipping sauce ingredients together until smooth.
- Serve fresh or fried rolls w/sauce + crushed peanuts on top!

Fun Fact:

Spring Rolls symbolize prosperity in Asian cultures and are often eaten during celebrations!

Thematic Tie-In:

Just like America's diverse history, these rolls blend flavors and textures from various cultures, proving that the best things come from unity and creativity!

Perfect Serving Occasions:

Light Lunches & Healthy Snacking
Party Appetizers & Potluck Favorites
Summertime Refreshments
DIY Asian-Themed Dinners

Drink Pairing:

Thai Iced Tea or Lemon Ginger Sparkling Water
Crisp Sauvignon Blanc or Rosé
Light Sake or Asian Lager

Ingredient Substitution Options:

No Shrimp? Use shredded chicken, tofu, or all veggies!

Gluten-Free? Use tamari instead of soy sauce.

Spicy? Add chili flakes or sriracha to the sauce!

Extra Creamy? Add avocado for a smooth contrast.

DIY Presentation & Decorating Ideas:

Arrange rolls in a circular pattern on a platter for a beautiful display.

Garnish with fresh herbs and sesame seeds for a restaurant-style touch.

Serve with chopsticks and small dipping bowls for an authentic feel!

Ingredient Storytelling:

Spring Rolls have traveled across borders, adapting to different cultures and tastes while maintaining their signature freshness and crunch. Like history itself, food evolves—each bite reminding us that new ideas can thrive while honoring tradition.

Zachary Taylor's Legacy:

As the 12th U.S. president (1849–1850), he never voted until he ran for president. He was a war hero known for his victories in the Mexican-American War. His presidency was brief, lasting only 16 months before his sudden death. A staunch nationalist, he opposed the expansion of slavery into new territories, angering Southern leaders despite being a slaveholder himself. His firm stance against secession helped delay the Civil War. Taylor's leadership style reflected his military background— decisive but politically inexperienced. Though he died before implementing major policies, his resistance to sectional tensions influenced later compromises. His legacy remains that of a soldier-president who prioritized unity over partisanship, setting a precedent for future leaders during America's most divisive era. See another version of this legacy on page 186.

What Core Value Shaped His Legacy?

Self-Reliance: Zachary Taylor wasn't a typical politician—he was a soldier who made choices based on what he thought was right, not what others told him to do. His story shows that sometimes, you have to make your own decisions and stick with them, even when it's hard.

Question: Have you ever had to make a tough choice without asking someone else what to do? How did it feel to figure it out on your own?

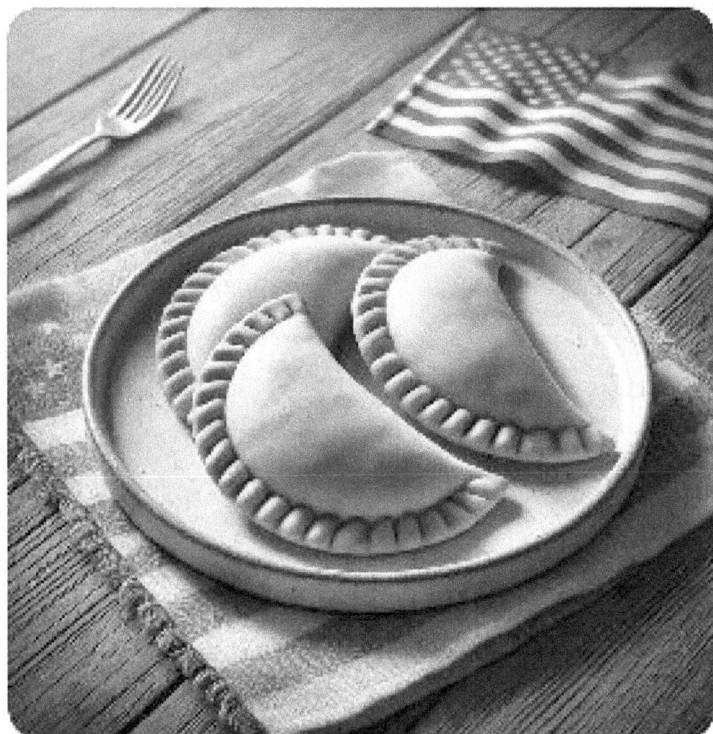

Chicken & Cheese Empanadas
Shredded Chicken and Gooey Cheese

It's America's Love for Hand-Held Foods

A crispy, golden-brown pastry stuffed with seasoned shredded chicken and gooey cheese. Perfect as a snack, appetizer, or main dish! These empanadas are a nod to the rich culinary heritage of Latin America while embracing the American love for comforting, handheld foods.

Warren Harding
"Like my 'Return to Normalcy,' these empanadas bring comfort and stability."

Servings: 12 | **Time:** 30 min | **Cook Time:** 20 min | Total Time: 50 min

For the Dough

- 3 cups all-purpose flour
- ½ teaspoon salt
- ½ cup unsalted butter, cold and diced
- 1 large egg
- ¾ cup cold water
- 1 tablespoon white vinegar

For the Filling

- 1 ½ cups cooked chicken, shredded
- ½ cup shredded Monterey Jack or cheddar cheese
- ½ small onion, finely chopped
- 1 clove garlic, minced
- ½ teaspoon ground cumin
- ½ teaspoon smoked paprika
- ¼ teaspoon chili powder (optional)
- Salt & black pepper, to taste
- 2 tablespoons tomato paste
- 2 tablespoons chicken broth
- 1 tablespoon olive oil

For Baking

- 1 egg, beaten (for egg wash)

Instructions to Bite Back Better*!*

Step 1: Prepare the Dough

- In a large bowl, mix the flour and salt.
- Cut in the butter using a pastry cutter or fork until the mixture resembles coarse crumbs.

- In a separate bowl, whisk together the egg, cold water, and vinegar. Gradually add to the flour mixture, stirring until a dough forms.
- Knead the dough on a lightly floured surface for 5 minutes until smooth. Wrap in plastic wrap and refrigerate for at least 30 minutes.

Step 2: Make the Filling

- Heat olive oil in a skillet over medium heat.
- Add onion and garlic, sauté until softened.
- Stir in shredded chicken, tomato paste, broth, cumin, smoked paprika, chili powder, salt, and pepper. Cook for 3-5 minutes until well combined.
- Remove from heat and let cool slightly before mixing in the shredded cheese.

Step 3: Assemble the Empanadas

- Preheat oven to 375°F (190°C). Line a baking sheet with parchment paper.
- Roll out the dough on a floured surface to about ⅛-inch thickness. Cut into 4-5 inch circles.
- Place 1-2 tablespoons of filling in the center of each circle.
- Fold the dough over the filling, forming a half-moon shape. Press the edges together and crimp with a fork or twist for a traditional look.
- Brush the tops with the beaten egg.

Step 4: Bake the Empanadas

- Arrange empanadas on the prepared baking sheet.
- Bake for 18-22 minutes, or until golden brown.
- Let cool slightly before serving.

Perfect Serving Suggestions

- Serve warm with chimichurri sauce, sour cream, or homemade guacamole.
- Pair with a side salad or black beans and rice for a complete meal.
- Cut into halves and serve as a party appetizer with a dipping station.

Drink Pairing

- **Kids:** Pair with a homemade limeade or fresh mango juice for a tropical twist.
- **Adults:** A light beer, sparkling sangria, or a spicy margarita complements the flaky crust and savory filling.

Fun Fact

Empanadas date back to medieval Spain, they traveled across the Atlantic with Spanish explorers and became a beloved dish across Latin America.

DIY Presentation & Decorating Ideas

- **Patriotic Touch:** Use a fork to create a crimped flag-like edge, or cut star shapes into the dough before baking.
- **Serving Board:** Arrange empanadas on a wooden board with dips in small bowls for an inviting presentation.
- **Dough Design:** Brush the tops with paprika-infused egg wash for a golden, slightly smoky finish.

Warren Harding's Legacy:

Elected in 1920, he championed his **"Return to Normalcy"** agenda, promoting pro-business policies, tax cuts, and reduced government intervention, which fueled economic growth; however, his administration was plagued by corruption, most notably the **Teapot Dome Scandal**, which tarnished his reputation after his sudden death in 1923. Despite scandals, Harding is remembered for restoring national confidence after World War I and laying the groundwork for the **Roaring Twenties**.

What Core Value Was Missing From His Legacy?

Integrity: Warren Harding was well-liked and wanted to bring calm after a difficult time in history. But he chose friends and advisors who abused their power, and he didn't step in to stop it. His story reminds us that ignoring wrong choices can hurt your reputation and your country.

Question: Why is it important to speak up or take action when you know something's wrong? What can happen if you stay silent just to keep the peace?

Mini Tacos
Big flavor in a small bite!

Perfect for Sharing

Rutherford B. Hayes
"I won the presidency by one electoral vote—let's hope no one votes against seconds!"

Big flavor in a small bite! These mini tacos are perfect for parties, snacks, or fun family dinners. Crispy shells filled with seasoned meat, melty cheese, and fresh toppings make them irresistible!

Servings: 20 Minis Tacos
Prep Time: 20 min | **Cook Time:** 15 min

For the Taco Shells

- 10 small corn tortillas (cut in half)
- 2 tablespoons vegetable oil

For the Filling

- 1 pound ground beef or shredded chicken
- ½ small onion, finely chopped
- 2 cloves garlic, minced
- 1 teaspoon ground cumin
- 1 teaspoon smoked paprika
- ½ teaspoon chili powder
- ½ teaspoon salt
- ¼ teaspoon black pepper
- ½ cup tomato sauce
- ¼ cup water
- 1 tablespoon olive oil

For the Toppings

- ½ cup shredded cheddar or Monterey Jack cheese
- ½ cup shredded lettuce
- ¼ cup diced tomatoes
- ¼ cup sour cream
- ¼ cup guacamole
- ¼ cup chopped fresh cilantro
- 1 lime, cut into wedges

Instructions to Bite Back Better*!*

Step 1: Prepare the Mini Taco Shells

- Preheat oven to 375°F (190°C).
- Cut small tortillas in half. Lightly brush both sides with vegetable oil.
- Drape over the edges of a muffin tin or tuck into the wells to create a taco shape.
- Bake for 8-10 minutes, until crispy and golden. Set aside.

Step 2: Cook the Filling

- Heat olive oil in a skillet over medium heat.
- Add onions and garlic; sauté until softened.
- Add ground beef or chicken, breaking it apart as it browns.
- Stir in cumin, smoked paprika, chili powder, salt, and pepper.
- Add tomato sauce and water, simmering for 5 minutes until thickened. Remove from heat.

Step 3: Assemble the Mini Tacos

- Fill each mini taco shell with a spoonful of meat.
- Sprinkle with shredded cheese while warm so it melts.
- Top with lettuce, tomatoes, sour cream, guacamole, and cilantro.
- Serve with lime wedges on the side.

Perfect Serving Suggestions

- Pair with **fresh salsa** or a **side of black beans and rice**.
- Serve with a **mini taco bar** so guests can add their own toppings.
- Offer a **variety of hot sauces** for spice lovers.

Drink Pairing

- **Kids:** Refreshing homemade watermelon agua fresca or limeade.
- **Teens:** A chilled sparkling lemonade or iced hibiscus tea.
- **Adults:** A classic margarita, spicy michelada, or a light Mexican beer like Modelo or Pacifico pairs perfectly with these flavorful tacos.

Fun Fact Tacos have been a part of Mexican cuisine for centuries, but mini tacos have become a modern favorite at food trucks and restaurants across America. Their small size makes them perfect for sharing and sampling different flavors.

Thematic Tie-In: A Bite-Sized American Tradition

Just like America's diverse culture, mini tacos represent a fusion of traditions—bringing people together over bold flavors and shared experiences. Whether served at a 4th of July cookout, Super Bowl party, or casual gathering, they remind us that great things come in small packages.

Ingredient Substitution Options

- **Protein:** Swap beef for ground turkey, pork, or black beans for a vegetarian option.
- **Dairy-Free:** Use dairy-free cheese and avocado cream.
- **Low-Carb:** Substitute mini lettuce cups instead of tortillas.

DIY Presentation & Decorating Ideas

- **Patriotic Flair:** Serve mini tacos on a red, white, and blue platter.
- **Taco Stand:** Use a wooden tray or mini taco holders for a stylish presentation.
- **Dipping Station:** Offer small bowls of queso, salsa, and guacamole for an interactive experience.

3 Rutherford B. Hayes traits, each paired with a quote that can inspire you to build strong character:

1. Integrity Over Popularity
"He serves his party best who serves his country best."
— Integrity means doing what's right, even if it's not what's popular.

2. Commitment to Education
"Universal education is the source of progress and reform."
— A reminder that learning is the key to personal and national success.

3. Courageous Restraint
"Do not let your peace depend on the words of men."
— True strength is shown through calm, steady leadership in tense moments.

Check out page 82 for his legacy description.

What Core Value Shaped His Legacy?
Integrity: Rutherford B. Hayes took office in a cloud of controversy, but he didn't let that define him. He made fair hiring a priority and refused to hand out jobs just to please political friends. His actions showed that real honesty means staying true to your word—even when it's not easy.
Question: Have you ever had to prove yourself by doing what's right instead of what's popular? How did it feel to stand by your decision?

Dumplings
(Potstickers)

Possible Main Dish

George H. W. Bush
"A little diplomacy, a little seasoning, and a perfect result!"

Crispy on the bottom, tender on top, and packed with savory goodness! These homemade potstickers are a perfect balance of texture and flavor, making them an irresistible appetizer or main dish.

Servings: 24 | **Prep Time:** 30 min | **Cook Time:** 15 min

For the Dumpling Dough (Optional, If Making from Scratch)

- 2 cups all-purpose flour
- ¾ cup warm water
- ½ teaspoon salt

For the Filling

- ½ pound ground pork or chicken
- ½ cup finely chopped napa cabbage
- 2 green onions, finely chopped
- 1 clove garlic, minced
- 1 teaspoon fresh ginger, grated
- 1 tablespoon soy sauce
- 1 teaspoon sesame oil
- ½ teaspoon salt
- ¼ teaspoon black pepper

For Cooking

- 2 tablespoons vegetable oil
- ½ cup water

For Dipping Sauce

- 2 tablespoons soy sauce
- 1 tablespoon rice vinegar
- ½ teaspoon sesame oil
- ½ teaspoon chili flakes (optional)
- ½ teaspoon sugar

Instructions to Bite Back Better*!*

Step 1: Prepare the Dumpling Dough (If Making from Scratch)

- In a large bowl, mix flour and salt.
- Slowly add warm water, stirring until a dough forms.

- Knead on a floured surface for about 5 minutes until smooth.
- Cover and let rest for 30 min while you prepare the filling.

Step 2: Make the Filling

- In a bowl, combine ground pork (or chicken), cabbage, green onions, garlic, ginger, soy sauce, sesame oil, salt, and pepper.
- Mix well until fully combined.

Step 3: Assemble the Dumplings

- Roll out dough and cut into 3-inch circles (or use store-bought dumpling wrappers).
- Place a small spoonful of filling in the center of each wrapper.
- Wet the edges with water, fold in half, and pinch to seal, pleating the edges for a traditional look.

Step 4: Cook the Potstickers

- Heat 1 tablespoon of oil in a non-stick skillet over medium heat.
- Arrange dumplings in a single layer, flat side down. Cook for 2-3 minutes until the bottoms are golden brown.
- Add ½ cup water, cover, and steam for 5-6 minutes until the filling is cooked through.
- Uncover and cook for another 1-2 minutes until the water evaporates and the bottoms are crispy.

Step 5: Make the Dipping Sauce

- In a small bowl, mix soy sauce, rice vinegar, sesame oil, sugar, and chili flakes.
- Serve alongside warm dumplings.

Perfect Serving Suggestions

- Serve with a side of steamed jasmine rice and stir-fried vegetables.
- Pair with a refreshing cucumber salad or hot and sour soup.
- Make it a meal by adding a side of miso soup or edamame.

Drink Pairing

- **Kids:** Try a lightly sweetened iced green tea or homemade lemonade.
- **Adults:** Pair with a crisp white wine, sake, or a light lager to complement the savory flavors.

Fun Fact: Dumplings have been a staple in Chinese cuisine for over 1,800 years! Originally eaten during Lunar New Year, they symbolize wealth and prosperity, as their shape resembles ancient gold ingots.

Ingredient Substitution Options

- **Protein:** Swap pork for chicken, shrimp, tofu, or mushrooms.
- **Gluten-Free:** Use rice paper or gluten-free wrappers.
- **Spicy Kick:** Add chopped chili peppers or Sriracha to the filling.

DIY Presentation & Decorating Ideas

- **Dumpling Platter:** Arrange dumplings in a circle with dipping sauce in the center.
- **Garnish:** Sprinkle with sesame seeds and chopped green onions.
- **Chopsticks Display:** Serve on a wooden board with chopsticks for an authentic feel.

George H. W. Bush's Legacy:

As the 41st President of the United States, he was known for his diplomacy and steady hand in global affairs. His greatest achievements include navigating the end of the Cold War, fostering international coalitions during the Gulf War, and signing the Americans with Disabilities Act. Bush emphasized global cooperation and a kinder, gentler nation. His presidency was marked by integrity, experience, and a commitment to public service. Even after his term, he continued humanitarian efforts, leaving a legacy of leadership and dedication to his country.

Author's Note: Read why I spent 15 minutes alone with him in my NH office, found in my book, *Laughing With Leaders.*

What Core Value Shaped His Legacy?

Service: George H. W. Bush dedicated nearly his entire life to helping others. He believed in putting the country before himself and often made choices based on duty, not popularity. He showed that real service lasts a lifetime.

Question: Have you ever helped someone or done the right thing even when no one noticed? Why does serving others matter, even when there's nothing in it for you?

Bruschetta
A classic Italian appetizer

Simplest yet most Beloved Italian Dish

A classic Italian appetizer, bruschetta is a simple yet flavorful dish featuring crispy toasted bread topped with a fresh tomato and basil mixture. Perfect for parties, gatherings, or as a light snack!

Servings: 6 | **Prep Time:** 15 min | **Cook Time:** 5 min

Zackary Taylor
"I kept the Union together —just like this bruschetta!"

For the Bruschetta Topping
- 4 ripe Roma tomatoes, diced
- 2 tablespoons fresh basil, chopped
- 1 clove garlic, minced
- 1 tablespoon extra virgin olive oil
- 1 teaspoon balsamic vinegar
- ¼ teaspoon salt
- ¼ teaspoon black pepper

For the Bread
- 1 baguette, sliced into ½-inch thick pieces
- 2 tablespoons olive oil
- 1 clove garlic, whole (for rubbing)

Instructions to Bite Back Better!

Step 1: Prepare the Tomato Topping
- In a bowl, combine diced tomatoes, chopped basil, minced garlic, olive oil, balsamic vinegar, salt, and pepper.
- Mix well and let sit for at least 10 minutes to allow the flavors to blend.

Step 2: Toast the Bread
- Preheat oven to 400°F (200°C) or heat a grill pan over medium heat.
- Arrange baguette slices on a baking sheet. Brush both sides lightly with olive oil.
- Toast for 4-5 minutes until golden and crispy.
- While warm, rub each slice with the whole garlic clove for extra flavor.

Step 3: Assemble the Bruschetta
- Spoon the tomato mixture onto each toasted baguette slice.
- Drizzle with additional olive oil if desired.
- Serve immediately and enjoy!

Perfect Serving Suggestions

- Pair with a side of fresh mozzarella or burrata for extra creaminess.
- Serve alongside a crisp garden salad or antipasto platter.
- Enjoy with grilled meats or seafood for a complete meal.

Drink Pairing

- **Kids:** Refreshing lemonade or sparkling water with mint.
- **Adults:** A light Pinot Grigio, Chianti, or a classic Aperol Spritz complements the flavors beautifully.

Fun Fact: Bruschetta dates back to 15th-century Italy, where olive farmers would toast bread and drizzle it with fresh olive oil to test its quality—creating one of the simplest yet most beloved Italian dishes!

Thematic Tie-In: The Power of Simplicity

Just like America's greatest values—hard work, tradition, and fresh ideas—bruschetta is built on simple, quality ingredients that stand the test of time.

Ingredient Substitution Options

- **Tomatoes:** Swap for **roasted red peppers or avocado** for a twist.
- **Bread:** Try whole wheat, sourdough, or gluten-free options.
- **Dairy Boost:** Add grated Parmesan or crumbled feta on top.

DIY Presentation & Decorating Ideas

- **Rustic Charm:** Serve on a wooden cutting board with fresh basil leaves.
- **Mini Bruschetta Bites:** Use small crostini rounds for bite-sized appetizers.
- **Drizzle It Up:** Add a swirl of balsamic glaze or truffle oil for extra flair.

Ingredient Storytelling: A Taste of Tradition
Bruschetta represents the essence of Italian cuisine—simple, fresh, and meant to be shared. Like a great conversation or a good book, it's the small things that bring the most joy.

A Thought for America's Youth

Taylor's life teaches young people the value of integrity, perseverance, and duty. He rose to leadership through hard work and resilience, proving that actions matter more than words. His ability to stand firm in times of division reminds us that courage in the face of uncertainty is what shapes true leaders with character.

Zachary Taylor's Legacy:

His legacy is defined by his unwavering commitment to national unity and his leadership during a pivotal time in American history. A career military officer, Taylor earned the nickname "Old Rough and Ready" for his fearless and pragmatic approach on the battlefield. His victories in the Mexican-American War made him a national hero, leading to his election as the 12th President of the United States in 1848. Though his presidency was short-lived, Taylor stood firmly against the expansion of slavery into new territories, a stance that helped shape future debates leading to the Civil War. See another version on page 170.

Check out page 170 for a description of his core value.

Falafel Balls with Dip

Popular Vegetarian Street Food

Joe Biden
"You know what bites back better? These falafel balls!"

Crispy on the outside, soft and flavorful on the inside—these homemade falafel balls are packed with herbs, spices, and chickpea goodness. Paired with a creamy tahini dip, they make the perfect appetizer, snack, or main dish!

Servings: 20 balls | **Prep Time:** 20 min (plus soaking time) | **Cook Time:** 15 min

For the Falafel Balls

- 1 ½ cups dried chickpeas (soaked overnight)
- ½ small onion, chopped
- 2 cloves garlic, minced
- ½ cup fresh parsley, chopped
- ½ cup fresh cilantro, chopped
- 1 teaspoon ground cumin
- 1 teaspoon ground coriander
- ½ teaspoon smoked paprika
- ½ teaspoon salt
- ¼ teaspoon black pepper
- ¼ teaspoon baking soda
- 1 tablespoon lemon juice
- 1 tablespoon flour (or chickpea flour for gluten-free)
- 2 tablespoons sesame seeds (optional)
- 2 tablespoons olive oil (for brushing, if baking)
- Vegetable oil (for frying)

For the Tahini Dip

- ½ cup tahini
- 2 tablespoons lemon juice
- 1 clove garlic, minced
- 2 tablespoons water (adjust for consistency)
- ½ teaspoon salt
- ¼ teaspoon ground cumin

Instructions to Bite Back Better!

Step 1: Prepare the Falafel Mixture

- Drain and rinse the soaked chickpeas. Pat dry with a paper towel.
- In a food processor, combine chickpeas, onion, garlic, parsley, cilantro, cumin, coriander, paprika, salt, pepper, baking soda, lemon juice, and flour.

- Pulse until the mixture is well combined but still slightly coarse.
- Transfer to a bowl, cover, and refrigerate for at least 30 minutes.

Step 2: Shape the Falafel Balls

- Using your hands or a small scoop, form the mixture into 1-inch balls.
- If baking, preheat the oven to 400°F (200°C) and place falafel balls on a parchment-lined tray. Brush lightly with olive oil.

Step 3: Cook the Falafel

- **Frying Method:** Heat 2 inches of vegetable oil in a pan over medium heat. Fry falafel balls for 3-4 minutes, turning occasionally, until golden brown. Drain on paper towels.
- **Baking Method:** Bake for 20-25 minutes, flipping halfway, until crispy and golden brown.
- **Air-Frying Method:** Air-fry at 375°F (190°C) for 12-15 minutes, shaking the basket halfway.

Step 4: Make the Tahini Dip

- In a small bowl, whisk together tahini, lemon juice, garlic, water, salt, and cumin.
- Adjust the consistency with more water if needed.

Step 5: Serve & Enjoy

- Serve warm falafel balls with tahini dip on the side.
  - Garnish with extra parsley and sesame seeds.

Perfect Serving Suggestions

- Serve in pita bread with lettuce, tomatoes, cucumbers, and tzatziki.
- Pair with a Mediterranean mezze platter featuring hummus, olives, and feta.
- Enjoy over a grain bowl with quinoa, roasted veggies, and lemon dressing.

Drink Pairing

- **Kids:** Refreshing mint lemonade or iced herbal tea.
- **Adults:** A light white wine like Sauvignon Blanc or chilled cucumber-infused water.

Fun Fact: Falafel is believed to have originated in ancient Egypt, made from fava beans before chickpeas became the star ingredient. Today, it's a staple in Middle Eastern cuisine and a popular vegetarian street food worldwide.

Thematic Tie-In: Strength in SimplicityLike the diverse cultures of America, falafel takes simple ingredients and transforms them into something bold, flavorful, and full of history—a reminder that greatness comes from humble beginnings.

Ingredient Substitution Options
- **No Chickpeas?** Use fava beans for an Egyptian-style falafel.
- **Gluten-Free?** Swap flour for chickpea flour or oat flour.
- **Spicy Kick?** Add ½ teaspoon cayenne or red pepper flakes.

DIY Presentation & Decorating Ideas
- **Falafel Cone:** Serve in a paper cone for a fun, street-food style experience.
- **Dipping Platter:** Arrange falafel balls in a circle with tahini dip in the center.
- **Garnish:** Sprinkle with sesame seeds, pomegranate arils, or fresh herbs.

Joe Biden's Legacy:
In his best-selling book, *Confronting the Presidents* (page 399), Bill O'Reilly, the world's best-selling historian, concludes, "...I believe Joe Biden is the second-worst performing president in history, only behind fellow Pennsylvanian James Buchanan." Since history is a never-ending argument, you can always disagree with someone else's set of arguments - even O'Reilly's - with your own set.

What Core Value Was Missing From His Legacy?
Accountability: During Joe Biden's presidency, his staff admitted to trying to hide his cognitive decline, and millions watching from home could already tell something was wrong; the nation was left wondering who was truly leading. Holding a title isn't the same as owning the role. Accountability means showing up fully, being honest about your capacity, and taking responsibility, especially when it's uncomfortable.

Parent: When things at home get tough, how do you show your kids what real accountability looks like?

Teen: What does it mean to own your role, even when it's easier to blame someone else or stay quiet?

Arancini (Risotto Balls)

A Crispy Bite of History

Bites of Sicily

Crispy on the outside, creamy and cheesy on the inside—these Italian rice balls are a perfect appetizer, snack, or party dish. A golden, deep-fried delight, arancini are made from risotto, stuffed with gooey mozzarella, and served with marinara sauce.

Servings: 16 | **Prep Time:** 25 min | Cook Time: 25 min

William Howard Taft
"I built a stronger Supreme Court—just like a well-made arancini!"

For the Risotto
- 1 cup arborio rice
- 2 ½ cups chicken or vegetable broth, warmed
- ½ small onion, finely chopped
- 2 tablespoons unsalted butter
- ½ cup grated Parmesan cheese
- ½ teaspoon salt
- ¼ teaspoon black pepper

For the Arancini
- ½ cup mozzarella cheese, cut into small cubes
- ½ cup all-purpose flour
- 2 large eggs, beaten
- 1 cup Italian-style breadcrumbs
- ½ teaspoon salt
- ¼ teaspoon black pepper
- ½ teaspoon garlic powder (optional)
- ½ teaspoon dried oregano (optional)
- Vegetable oil, for frying

For Serving
- 1 cup marinara sauce, warmed
- Fresh basil or parsley, for garnish

Instructions to Bite Back Better!

Step 1: Make the Risotto
- In a saucepan, melt butter over medium heat. Add chopped onion and sauté until soft.
- Stir in arborio rice and cook for 1 min until lightly toasted.
- Gradually add warm broth, ½ cup at a time, stirring constantly until absorbed. Continue this process until the rice is tender and creamy (about 20 minutes).

- Stir in Parmesan cheese, salt, and pepper. Let cool completely (refrigerating for at least 1 hour speeds up the process).

Step 2: Shape the Arancini

- Take a spoonful of cooled risotto and flatten it in your palm.
- Place a cube of mozzarella in the center and wrap the risotto around it, forming a ball.
- Repeat with remaining rice and cheese.
- **Step 3: Coat the Arancini**
- Prepare three bowls:
  - **Bowl 1:** Flour
  - **Bowl 2:** Beaten eggs
  - **Bowl 3:** Breadcrumbs mixed with salt, pepper, garlic powder, and oregano.
- Roll each rice ball in flour, dip in egg, then coat with breadcrumbs.

Step 4: Fry the Arancini

- Heat 2 inches of vegetable oil in a deep pan to 350°F (175°C).
- Fry arancini in batches, turning occasionally, until golden brown (about 3-4 minutes).
- Drain on paper towels.

Step 5: Serve & Enjoy

- Serve warm with marinara sauce for dipping.
- Garnish with fresh basil or parsley.

Perfect Serving Suggestions

- Serve with a side of garlic aioli or pesto for dipping.
- Pair with a light salad for a balanced meal.
- Enjoy as a party appetizer with a variety of sauces.

Drink Pairing

- **Kids:** Refreshing sparkling lemonade or Italian soda.
- **Adults:** A light Pinot Grigio or classic Aperol Spritz complements the crispy, cheesy goodness.

Fun Fact: Arancini originated in Sicily and were named after "arancia" (orange) due to their round, golden appearance. They were originally created as a way to use up leftover risotto!

Thematic Tie-In: Tradition Meets Innovation

Just like America, arancini combine old-world flavors with new ideas—a crispy bite of history that continues to evolve!

Ingredient Substitution Options

- **Cheese:** Swap mozzarella for fontina or provolone.
- **Gluten-Free:** Use gluten-free flour and breadcrumbs.
- **Baked Version:** Bake at 400°F (200°C) for 20-25 minutes, turning halfway.

DIY Presentation & Decorating Ideas

- **Elegant Serving:** Stack arancini in a pyramid with marinara drizzle.
- **Party Style:** Serve in small paper cones for a grab-and-go snack.
- **Gourmet Touch:** Sprinkle with truffle salt or grated Parmesan.

Ingredient Storytelling: A Bite of Sicily

From Sicilian street vendors to fine dining, arancini have stood the test of time, proving that great food is all about tradition, creativity, and a little bit of crunch.

William Howard Taft's Legacy:

His legacy is one of dedication, reform, and lasting impact on the American legal system. As the 27th President of the United States and later the 10th Chief Justice of the Supreme Court, he remains the only person to have held both offices. As president, Taft focused on trust-busting, breaking up monopolies to ensure fair business competition. He also expanded civil service protections, ensuring government jobs were awarded based on merit. Taft teaches young people that persistence and growth matter—even after being voted out of office, he found his true calling in law and left an even greater impact. His life proves that setbacks aren't failures—*they're opportunities* to find where you truly belong.

What Core Value Shaped His Legacy?
Respect: William Howard Taft deeply valued the Constitution, the law, and the structure of government. Even as president, he believed no one was above the rules—not even himself. Later, as Chief Justice, he proved that respecting the law and the process was more important than chasing power or popularity.
Question: Why is it important to respect rules and fairness, even when it's not convenient? How does that help others trust you and the decisions you make?

Mini Samosas
Crispy with Stuffed Delights

A Blend of Global Flavors

Crispy, golden, and packed with flavorful spiced filling, these mini samosas are perfect for parties, snacks, or festive gatherings. Serve them with chutney or yogurt dip for an irresistible treat!

Servings: 20 | **Prep Time:** 30 min | **Cook Time:** 20 min

Barack Obama
"Yes we can... have more samosas!"

For the Dough

- 1 cup all-purpose flour
- 2 tablespoons oil or melted butter
- ¼ teaspoon salt
- ¼ cup water (as needed)

For the Filling

- 1 medium potato, boiled and mashed
- ½ cup green peas (boiled or frozen)
- ½ small onion, finely chopped
- 1 clove garlic, minced
- ½ teaspoon cumin seeds
- ½ teaspoon garam masala
- ½ teaspoon turmeric powder
- ½ teaspoon coriander powder
- ¼ teaspoon red chili powder (optional)
- ½ teaspoon salt
- 1 tablespoon oil
- 1 tablespoon fresh cilantro, chopped (optional)

For Frying

- Vegetable oil, for deep frying

Instructions to Bite Back Better!

Step 1: Prepare the Dough

- In a bowl, mix flour, salt, and oil/butter until crumbly.
- Gradually add water and knead into a firm dough. Cover and rest for 20 minutes.

Step 2: Make the Filling
- Heat oil in a pan, add cumin seeds, and let them sizzle.
- Add onions and garlic, sauté until soft.
- Stir in mashed potatoes, peas, and all spices. Cook for 2-3 minutes.
- Remove from heat and let cool.

Step 3: Shape the Samosas
- Divide the dough into small balls and roll each into a thin oval.
- Cut in half to form two semi-circles.
- Fold into a cone, sealing the edges with water.
- Fill with 1 teaspoon of stuffing and seal tightly.

Step 4: Cook the Samosas
- **Frying Method:** Heat oil to 350°F (175°C) and fry until golden brown, about 3-4 minutes per batch.
- **Baking Method:** Preheat oven to 375°F (190°C), brush samosas with oil, and bake for 20-25 minutes.
- **Air-Frying Method:** Air-fry at 375°F (190°C) for 12-15 minutes, shaking halfway through.

Step 5: Serve & Enjoy
- Serve warm with green chutney, tamarind sauce, or spicy yogurt dip.

Perfect Serving Suggestions
- Pair with a cup of masala chai for an authentic experience.
- Serve as part of a mezze platter with other snacks.
- Arrange with sliced cucumbers and mint yogurt for a refreshing touch.

Drink Pairing
- **Kids:** Sweet mango lassi or lemonade.
- **Adults:** A spiced chai latte or light beer.

Fun Fact: Samosas originated in the Middle East and traveled to India, Africa, and beyond, evolving into the crispy, stuffed delights we know today!

Ingredient Substitution Options
- **No Potatoes?** Use chickpeas or paneer instead.
- **Gluten-Free?** Use rice flour or almond flour for the dough.
- **Spicy Kick?** Add finely chopped green chilies to the filling.

DIY Presentation & Decorating Ideas
- **Stacked Samosa Tower:** Arrange samosas in a pyramid for a fun presentation.
- **Mini Dipping Station:** Serve with three sauces in colorful bowls.
- **Garnish:** Sprinkle with pomegranate seeds and chopped mint for extra flair.

Barack Obama's Legacy:
He ran for president with the message of "hope and change." But once he was in office, some things turned out differently than expected. Unexpected conversations about race became louder and more intense. Some people felt he helped bring attention to important issues, while others believed his approach made people feel more divided. The national debt, the money the government owes, almost doubled while he was in office. Some said this was necessary to deal with economic problems, but others worried about how much the country was spending. One of his dubious accomplishments was the Affordable Care Act. Many families saw their insurance costs go up and had fewer choices for doctors and plans. Obama was re-elected for a second term, helped by eloquent speeches and a well-organized campaign. People still debate his legacy. Some believe he made lasting progress, while others feel his policies caused new problems.

What Core Value Was Missing From His Legacy?

Integrity: Barack Obama inspired millions with messages of unity and change. But some of his biggest promises—like affordable healthcare and reducing racial division—didn't match what many Americans experienced. His story reminds us that integrity means keeping your word and staying consistent between what you say and what you do.

Question: Why do you think it's easy to make promises but harder to keep them? What does it take to be the kind of person others can count on, even when things get tough?

Chicken Satay Skewers
With Peanut Sauce

A Street-Food Favorite

Jimmy Carter
"Bringing flavors together
—just like I did with peace
at Camp David."

Juicy, marinated chicken skewers grilled to perfection and served with a creamy, flavorful peanut sauce. This Southeast Asian classic makes for a perfect appetizer, party snack, or main dish!

Servings: 4 (about 12 skewers)

Prep Time: 20 min (plus 30 min marination) | **Cook Time:** 10 min

For the Chicken Skewers

- 1 pound boneless, skinless chicken breast or thighs, cut into thin strips
- 12 wooden skewers (soaked in water for 30 minutes)

For the Marinade

- 2 tablespoons soy sauce
- 1 tablespoon lime juice
- 1 tablespoon honey or brown sugar
- 1 tablespoon vegetable oil
- 2 cloves garlic, minced
- 1 teaspoon grated fresh ginger
- 1 teaspoon turmeric powder
- ½ teaspoon ground cumin
- ½ teaspoon chili flakes (optional)
- ½ teaspoon salt

For the Peanut Sauce

- ¼ cup peanut butter (creamy or chunky)
- 2 tablespoons soy sauce
- 1 tablespoon lime juice
- 1 tablespoon honey or brown sugar
- ½ teaspoon grated ginger
- ½ teaspoon chili flakes (optional)
- ¼ cup coconut milk or water (adjust for consistency)

Instructions to Bite Back Better!

Step 1: Marinate the Chicken

- In a bowl, mix all marinade ingredients until well combined.
- Add chicken strips, toss to coat, and marinate for at least 30 minutes (or up to 2 hours for deeper flavor).

Step 2: Prepare the Peanut Sauce

- In a small saucepan over low heat, whisk together peanut butter, soy sauce, lime juice, honey, ginger, and chili flakes.
- Add coconut milk or water gradually until the sauce reaches a smooth, pourable consistency.
- Simmer for 2-3 minutes, then remove from heat.

Step 3: Grill the Skewers

- Grill: Preheat grill or grill pan over medium-high heat. Cook skewers for 3-4 minutes per side, until golden brown and cooked through.
- Oven: Broil at 450°F (230°C) for 8-10 minutes, flipping halfway.
- Stovetop: Heat a pan with 1 tablespoon oil and cook for 4-5 minutes per side.

Step 4: Serve & Enjoy

- Serve skewers with warm peanut sauce on the side.
- Garnish with chopped cilantro, crushed peanuts, and lime wedges.

Perfect Serving Suggestions

- Pair with steamed jasmine rice or coconut rice.
- Serve with cucumber salad or grilled vegetables.
- Add to a wrap or salad for a protein-packed meal.

Drink Pairing

- Kids: Fresh mango juice or iced lemon tea.
- Adults: Chilled Sauvignon Blanc or a light Thai beer.

Fun Fact: Chicken Satay originated in Indonesia but is now popular across Thailand, Malaysia, and beyond—a true street food favorite!

Thematic Tie-In: Bringing Cultures Together

Like America's diverse communities, satay blends global flavors into something everyone can enjoy.

Ingredient Substitution Options

- No Chicken? Try tofu, shrimp, or beef instead.
- Nut-Free? Replace peanut sauce with tahini or sunflower seed butter.
- Extra Spicy? Add more chili flakes or a splash of Sriracha.

DIY Presentation & Decorating Ideas

- Serving Board: Arrange skewers on a wooden board with dipping sauce in the center.
- Plating Tip: Serve skewers in a banana leaf-lined tray for an authentic touch.
- Garnish: Sprinkle with toasted sesame seeds and fresh mint
-

Jimmy Carter's Legacy:

As the 39th president of the United States, and a peanut farmer from Georgia, he showed that success isn't just about fame or power—it's about kindness, determination, and staying true to your values. Growing up in a small town in the South, Carter believed that doing the right thing mattered, even when no one was watching. As president, he made history by helping bring peace between Egypt and Israel through the **Camp David Accords**, showing that determination and understanding can solve even the toughest problems.

But Carter's story didn't end after his presidency. He dedicated his life to helping others, building homes with *Habitat for Humanity,* fighting diseases, and standing up for human rights around the world. His life reminds our youth that being compassionate, persistent, and caring for others can create real change. Carter proved that making a difference doesn't require power—just the courage to act with heart.

What Core Value Shaped His Legacy?

Service: Jimmy Carter believed in helping others—before, during, and long after his time as president. From promoting peace to building homes for those in need, he showed that real service isn't about titles—it's about action. His life reminds us that leadership doesn't stop when the job ends.

Question: What does it mean to serve others without expecting anything in return? How can you make service part of your everyday life?

Teriyaki Meat Skewers
Celebrating Unity on a Stick

Juicy, savory, and sweet

Juicy, savory, and sweet—these skewers unite flavors in perfect harmony.

Servings: 10 | **Prep Time:** 20 min | **Marinate Time:** 30 min | **Cook Time:** 15 min

Ulysses S. Grant
"I rebuilt unity; this skewer blends it perfectly."

For the Skewers:

- 2 lbs beef sirloin or chicken breast, cut into 1-inch cubes
- 1 red bell pepper, cut into chunks
- 1 yellow bell pepper, cut into chunks
- 1 zucchini, sliced into thick rounds
- 1 red onion, cut into chunks
- Wooden or metal skewers

For the Teriyaki Marinade:

- 1/2 cup soy sauce
- 1/4 cup honey
- 1/4 cup brown sugar
- 2 tablespoons rice vinegar
- 1 tablespoon sesame oil
- 2 cloves garlic, minced
- 1 tablespoon fresh ginger, grated
- 1 tablespoon cornstarch mixed with 2 tablespoons water (for thickening)
- Sesame seeds and chopped green onions, for garnish

Instructions to Bite Back Better!

1. **Prepare the Marinade:**
   In a saucepan, combine soy sauce, honey, brown sugar, rice vinegar, sesame oil, garlic, and ginger. Bring to a simmer over medium heat. Stir in the cornstarch mixture and cook until the sauce thickens (about 2 minutes). Let cool.

2. Marinate the Meat:
Place the meat cubes in a large bowl. Pour half of the cooled teriyaki sauce over the meat and toss to coat. Marinate for at least 30 minutes in the refrigerator.

3. Assemble the Skewers:
Thread the marinated meat, bell peppers, zucchini, and onion onto the skewers, alternating for a colorful presentation.

4. Grill the Skewers:
Preheat the grill to medium-high heat. Grill the skewers for 10-15 minutes, turning occasionally and brushing with the remaining teriyaki sauce until the meat is cooked through and has nice grill marks.

5. Garnish and Serve:
Sprinkle the skewers with sesame seeds and chopped green onions. Serve warm with extra teriyaki sauce on the side.

Drink Pairing:

- **Refreshing Option:** Sparkling lemonade with a hint of mint and lime complements the sweet and savory flavors.
- **For Adults:** A chilled glass of Pinot Noir or a crisp lager balances the teriyaki's richness.

DIY Presentation & Decorating Ideas:

- **Skewer Station:** Create a "Build Your Own Skewer" station with various veggies and meats.
- **Patriotic Touch:** Use star-shaped plates, red-white-and-blue napkins, and mini American flags on each skewer for a festive look.
- **Outdoor Vibe:** String fairy lights around the serving area for a warm, picnic feel.

Fun Facts:

- **Teriyaki Origins:** The word "teriyaki" comes from the Japanese words *teri* (glossy shine) and *yaki* (grill or broil).
- **Presidential Favorite:** Did you know that former President Ulysses S. Grant loved international cuisine during his world tour after leaving office? These skewers represent blending cultures—just like Grant built unity after the Civil War.

Ingredient Substitution Options:

- **Meat:** Swap beef/chicken for tofu, shrimp, or pork.
- **Sauce:** Try hoisin or sweet chili sauce for a different flavor.
- **Veggies:** Use mushrooms, pineapple chunks, or asparagus for more variety.

Thematic Tie-In: "Grilling for Unity"

These **Teriyaki Meat Skewers** combine sweet, savory, and smoky flavors into one delicious dish. Perfect for celebrating unity, freedom, and flavor—all on a single stick!

Ulysses S. Grant's Legacy:

He proved that determination and perseverance can lead to greatness. Grant wasn't the loudest voice in the room, but he believed in action. As a general, he led the Union Army to victory in the Civil War, refusing to give up even when times were tough. His leadership wasn't about glory —it was about bringing a divided nation back together. As the 18th president, Grant worked hard to protect the rights of newly freed people and fought for equality during Reconstruction. He believed that a nation could only be strong if everyone had a fair chance. Grant teaches today's youth that success doesn't come from taking the easy path—it comes from standing firm, making tough choices, and fighting for what's right. His story reminds us that true strength is found in unity, determination, and *never backing down from a challenge.*

What Core Value Shaped His Legacy?

Perseverance: Ulysses S. Grant faced failure, doubt, and hardship—but he kept going. From personal setbacks to leading the Union Army to victory, he showed grit when it mattered most. As president, he fought for civil rights during a tough and divided time. His story proves that steady effort can lead to lasting change.

Question: Have you ever wanted to give up on something difficult? What helped you keep going—and what did you learn from it?

Caprese Skewers
Tomato, Mozzarella, Basil

Simplicity and Quality

A fresh and vibrant appetizer, Caprese Skewers combine juicy cherry tomatoes, creamy mozzarella, and fragrant basil leaves, drizzled with balsamic glaze. Perfect for parties, picnics, or a light, refreshing snack!

Servings: 12 skewers | **Time:** 15 min | **Cook Time:** None

Andrew Johnson
"I stood for unity—just like these skewers!"

Ingredients

- 12 cherry or grape tomatoes
- 12 mini mozzarella balls (bocconcini or ciliegine)
- 12 fresh basil leaves
- 1 tablespoon extra virgin olive oil
- 1 tablespoon balsamic glaze (or balsamic reduction)
- ¼ teaspoon salt
- ¼ teaspoon black pepper
- 12 small wooden skewers or toothpicks

Instructions to Bite Back Better!

Step 1: Assemble the Skewers

- Take a skewer or toothpick and thread a cherry tomato, a fresh basil leaf, and a mini mozzarella ball.
- Repeat until all skewers are assembled, alternating the ingredients for a colorful presentation.

Step 2: Season & Dress

- Arrange the skewers on a serving platter.
- Drizzle with olive oil and balsamic glaze.
- Sprinkle lightly with salt and black pepper.

Step 3: Serve & Enjoy

- Serve immediately or refrigerate until ready to serve.
- Garnish with extra fresh basil leaves for a beautiful presentation.

Perfect Serving Suggestions

- Serve alongside a charcuterie board for a balanced appetizer spread.
- Pair with crusty bread or grissini (breadsticks).
- Add to a salad or pasta dish for extra flavor.

Drink Pairing

- **Kids:** Refreshing sparkling water with lemon or fruit-infused water.
- **Adults:** A crisp Pinot Grigio, Prosecco, or a light rosé complements the fresh flavors perfectly.

Fun Fact

The Caprese salad originated from the island of Capri, Italy, and its colors—red, white, and green—represent the Italian flag. These skewers are a fun twist on the classic dish!

Thematic Tie-In: Simple Ingredients, Big Impact

Just like the best American values, these skewers show that simple, quality ingredients can create something truly special.

Ingredient Substitution Options

- **Tomatoes:** Swap for grilled peppers or cucumber slices.
- **Cheese:** Use feta or goat cheese cubes instead of mozzarella.
- **Basil:** Replace with fresh mint or arugula for a different twist.

DIY Presentation & Decorating Ideas

- **Patriotic Flair:** Arrange skewers in the shape of an American flag using red tomatoes, white mozzarella, and green basil.
- **Appetizer Tower:** Serve on a tiered platter for an elegant presentation.
- **Dipping Option:** Provide a small bowl of balsamic glaze for dipping.

Ingredient Storytelling: A Taste of Italy

Caprese skewers bring the flavors of the Mediterranean to your table, proving that simplicity and quality are the keys to timeless dishes.

Andrew Johnson's Legacy:

He became the 17th President of the United States after Abraham Lincoln's assassination in 1865. His presidency came during Reconstruction, a challenging time when the country needed to rebuild after the Civil War. Johnson focused on reuniting the North and South, but his approach often clashed with Congress. He offered leniency to the South, which some felt did not do enough to protect the rights of newly freed slaves. His conflicts with Congress led to his impeachment, making him the first U.S. president to face this; however, he was not removed from office. Johnson's legacy is mixed—while he worked to bring the country back together, his policies on civil rights and Reconstruction were seen as controversial. Andrew Johnson's biggest failure was his lenient Reconstruction policies, opposing civil rights for freed slaves, and allowing restrictive "Black Codes" to emerge. His story teaches the importance of balance, leadership, and the challenges of healing a divided nation. Sadly, he didn't meet them.

What Core Value Was Missing From His Legacy?

Humility: Andrew Johnson took office after Lincoln's assassination but struggled to unite the country. He often refused advice, clashed with Congress, and acted with stubborn pride instead of openness. His story shows what can go wrong when a leader lacks humility and refuses to learn or listen.

Question: Why is it important to stay humble, especially when you're in charge? What can happen when someone refuses to listen or admit they're wrong?

Stuffed Mini Peppers
No Seeds, No Mess

Beautiful and Delicious

Bright, colorful, and packed with a delicious creamy filling, these stuffed mini peppers make the perfect appetizer, snack, or party dish. Easy to prepare and full of flavor, they're always a crowd-pleaser!

Servings: 24 **Time:** 20 min | **Cook Time:** 15 min

Ronald Reagan
"I brought down walls.
Now I'm filling peppers!"

For the Peppers

- 12 mini sweet peppers (multicolored)
- 1 tablespoon olive oil
- ¼ teaspoon salt
- ¼ teaspoon black pepper

- **For the Filling**

- 8 ounces cream cheese, softened
- ½ cup shredded cheddar cheese
- ¼ cup grated Parmesan cheese
- 2 tablespoons fresh chives, chopped
- 1 teaspoon garlic powder
- 1 teaspoon onion powder
- ½ teaspoon smoked paprika (optional)
- ½ teaspoon Italian seasoning
- ¼ teaspoon salt
- ¼ teaspoon black pepper

- **Optional Toppings**

- ¼ cup panko breadcrumbs (for a crunchy topping)
- 1 tablespoon melted butter
- Fresh herbs (chives, parsley) for garnish

- **Instructions to Bite Back Netter!**

- **Step 1: Prepare the Mini Peppers**

- Preheat oven to 400°F (200°C) and line a baking sheet with parchment paper.
- Slice mini peppers in half lengthwise, removing seeds and membranes.

- Toss peppers with olive oil, salt, and black pepper. Arrange cut side up on the baking sheet.

Fun Fact

Mini peppers are sweeter and milder than traditional bell peppers, making them a great snack for kids and adults alike—no seeds, no mess!

Thematic Tie-In: Bringing Color and Flavor Together

Like America's diverse communities, these stuffed mini peppers combine different flavors and colors to create a dish that is both beautiful and delicious.

Ingredient Substitution Options

- **Cheese:** Swap cheddar for feta or goat cheese.
- **Herbs:** Use **dill or basil** instead of chives.
- Low-Carb: Skip the panko topping for a keto-friendly **version**.

DIY Presentation & Decorating Ideas

- **Patriotic Flair:** Arrange peppers on a red, white, and blue platter for festive occasions.
- **Appetizer Skewers:** Thread filled peppers onto mini skewers for easy serving.
- **Garnish:** Add a sprinkle of paprika or fresh herbs for a colorful finish.

Ingredient Storytelling: A Bite of Sunshine

Stuffed mini peppers bring a burst of color and flavor to any meal, reminding us that good things often come in small packages.

Ronald Reagan's Legacy:
His legacy is a powerful reminder of the impact that optimism, resilience, and bold leadership can have on a nation and the world. As the 40th President of the United States, Reagan took office during a time of economic struggles and global tension. His vision for America was rooted in hope and opportunity, believing that with hard work and perseverance, anything was possible.

Reagan's economic policies, known as "Reaganomics," focused on lowering taxes, reducing government regulation, and promoting free enterprise. These changes helped revive the American economy, creating jobs and boosting confidence. He showed that big challenges could be overcome with innovative ideas and a can-do spirit.

On the world stage, Reagan was a champion of freedom and democracy. His "peace through strength" approach helped bring an end to the Cold War, and his famous call to "tear down this wall!" in Berlin symbolized his commitment to breaking down barriers. Reagan's ability to communicate effectively, earning him the nickname "The Great Communicator," helped unite Americans and inspire action.

For teens, Reagan's legacy teaches the importance of standing firm in your beliefs (aka character), leading with integrity, and knowing that one person's voice can make a difference.

Check out page 74 for five of his quotes reflecting character.

"Bringing people together, whether through leadership or stuffed peppers!"

Avocado Toast Bites
Combines Freshness With Crunch

"Alligator Pears"

Crispy, creamy, and packed with flavor—these avocado toast bites are the perfect appetizer, snack, or party dish. Easy to make and endlessly customizable, they're always a hit!

Servings: 12 bites | **Time:** 10 min | **Cook Time:** 5 min

Donald Trump
"When I eat avocado,
I win, and I win HUGE!"

For the Toast Bites

- 6 slices of baguette or mini bread, cut into bite-sized pieces
- 1 ripe avocado
- 1 tablespoon fresh lemon or lime juice
- 1 tablespoon extra virgin olive oil
- ½ teaspoon salt
- ¼ teaspoon black pepper

Optional Toppings

- Cherry tomatoes, halved
- Red pepper flakes
- Everything bagel seasoning
- Microgreens or fresh herbs (e.g., cilantro, parsley)
- Crumbled feta or goat cheese
- Balsamic glaze for drizzling

Instructions to Bite Back Better!

- **Step 1: Prepare the Bread**
- Lightly toast the bread slices in a toaster, oven, or on a skillet until golden and crispy.
- Brush with a bit of olive oil for extra flavor.

- **Step 2: Make the Avocado Spread**
In a bowl, mash the avocado with lemon juice, salt, and pepper until smooth but still a bit chunky.

Step 3: Assemble the Bites
- Spread a generous amount of mashed avocado on each toast bite.
- Add your favorite toppings, such as cherry tomatoes, red pepper flakes, microgreens, or cheese.

Step 4: Serve & Enjoy
Arrange on a platter, drizzle with olive oil or balsamic glaze, and serve immediately.

Perfect Serving Suggestions

- Pair with a fresh green salad for a light lunch.
- Serve alongside a charcuterie board for a colorful appetizer spread.
- Enjoy with poached eggs for a brunch twist.

Drink Pairing

- **Kids:** Refreshing sparkling water with cucumber or fruit-infused lemonade.
- **Adults:** A crisp Sauvignon Blanc or a light mimosa.

Fun Fact

Avocados are sometimes called "alligator pears" because of their bumpy green skin. They are also rich in healthy fats, vitamins, and minerals!

Thematic Tie-In: Simple, Fresh, and Flavorful

Like the best ideas, these avocado toast bites are proof that great things come from simple ingredients.

Ingredient Substitution Options

- **No Baguette?** Use crackers, pita chips, or cucumber slices.
- **Dairy-Free?** Skip the cheese or use dairy-free feta.
- **Spicy Kick?** Add a sprinkle of chili flakes or hot sauce.

DIY Presentation & Decorating Ideas

- **Patriotic Flair:** Arrange bites on a red, white, and blue platter for a festive touch.
- **Mini Skewers:** Serve on toothpicks for easy snacking.
- **Garnish:** Top with edible flowers or a sprinkle of everything bagel seasoning.

Ingredient Storytelling: A Bite of Freshness

Avocado toast bites combine freshness and crunch, reminding us that sometimes the simplest things bring the greatest joy.

Donald Trump's Legacy:
His legacy is defined by his focus on bold leadership, business acumen, and challenging the status quo.

As the 45th and 47th President of the United States, Trump brings a non-traditional approach to politics, drawing on his experience as a businessman and media personality. He emphasizes economic growth, promoting policies that aim to boost businesses, create jobs, and reduce taxes. His administration focuses on "America First," prioritizing national interests, promoting patriotism, and encouraging self-reliance and entrepreneurship.

Trump's emphasis on building confidence, thinking big, and taking calculated risks can inspire young people to pursue their goals fearlessly. His belief in hard work and perseverance is a reminder that setbacks are not the end, but a step toward success.

As the most publicly prosecuted figure in presidential history, along with two assassination attempts, Trump's ability to overcome long legal suits and win, to mobilize a strong base of supporters, create global business ventures, and navigate high-stakes negotiations demonstrate the power of *determination and self-belief.*

For today's youth, Trump's legacy highlights the importance of bold thinking, resilience, and staying true to one's vision, even when facing unjust criticism. His story encourages young people to embrace challenges, take initiative, and understand that leadership often requires standing firm in one's beliefs and making tough decisions.

What Core Value Shaped His Legacy?

Perseverance: Donald Trump faced nonstop challenges—from media attacks to legal battles—but stayed focused on his goals. He built a movement, led boldly, and didn't back down from tough situations. His story shows that perseverance means pushing forward, even when the odds are stacked against you.

Question: Have you ever had to keep going when everything felt stacked against you? What gave you the strength not to quit?

Fruit and Cheese Kabobs
Crisp Cool Bites

Terrific Hydrating Vegetable

Colorful, fresh, and perfectly snackable, Fruit and Cheese Kabobs are a fun and healthy treat for all ages. Easy to assemble and endlessly customizable, they're ideal for parties, lunchboxes, or patriotic-themed gatherings!

Abraham Lincoln
"Emancipate your taste buds, one kabob at a time."

Servings: 12 kabobs | **Time:** 15–20 min | **Cook Time:** None

Fruits *(choose a variety for color and flavor)*

- 1 cup red grapes
- 1 cup green grapes
- 1 cup strawberries, hulled and halved
- 1 cup pineapple chunks
- 1 apple, cubed and tossed in lemon juice to prevent browning
- 1 cup blueberries (for mini skewers or garnish)

Cheese *(cubed into ¾-inch pieces)*

- 1 cup cheddar cheese
- 1 cup Monterey Jack or Colby Jack
- 1 cup mozzarella (block-style or bocconcini balls, halved if large)

Optional Add-Ons

- Fresh mint leaves
- Honey drizzle
- Toothpicks or 6-inch wooden skewers

Instructions to Bite Back Better!

Step 1: Prepare the Ingredients

- Wash all fruit and dry thoroughly.
- Cube or slice fruits and cheeses into bite-sized pieces.

Step 2: Assemble the Kabobs

- On each skewer or toothpick, alternate fruit and cheese for color and balance. Example combo: strawberry, cheddar, grape, mozzarella, pineapple, Monterey Jack.
- Add a mint leaf between ingredients for freshness (optional).
- For mini kabobs, use toothpicks with 2–3 pieces per stick.

Step 3: Serve or Store

- Serve immediately or chill until ready to enjoy.
- Can be stored in an airtight container in the fridge for up to 24 hours.

Perfect Serving Suggestions

- Serve as a snack tray, appetizer, or brunch side.
- Pair with yogurt dip, chocolate drizzle, or a honey-balsamic glaze.
- Great for picnics, parties, patriotic events, or school lunches.

Drink Pairing

- **Kids:** Fruit punch, lemonade, or flavored water
- **Adults:** White wine (Riesling, Pinot Grigio) or a fruity sangria

Fun Fact

Fruit and cheese pairings date back to ancient Rome, where fresh grapes and hard cheeses were enjoyed for their contrast in flavor and texture. Some combos are just timeless!

Thematic Tie-In: Variety and Harmony

Just like a great team or nation, these kabobs show how different pieces come together to create something vibrant and delicious.

Ingredient Substitution Options

- **Fruit:** Swap in melon, kiwi, mango, or raspberries
- **Cheese:** Try brie cubes, gouda, or pepper jack for more variety
- **Vegan Option:** Use plant-based cheeses and add extra fruit like figs or dates

DIY Presentation & Decorating Ideas

- Arrange kabobs in the shape of a flag, star, or fruit rainbow
- Use red, white, and blue ingredients for July 4th (e.g., strawberries, blueberries, white cheddar)
- Place in a pineapple half or carved watermelon for tropical flair

Ingredient Storytelling: A Bite of Balance

These kabobs balance sweetness, saltiness, and freshness —a delicious reminder that the best things in life come in a mix of flavors.

The Legacy of Abraham Lincoln:

Abraham Lincoln's legacy offers more than just presidential achievement: *it's a masterclass in character for young people today:* check out pages 77-78. Lincoln wasn't just a great leader, he was also our most prolific presidential writer and, surprisingly to many, our most humorous. His speeches and letters were rich with wisdom, wit, and emotional depth, showing that clarity of thought and a sense of humor can coexist with serious leadership. In just 272 words, his Gettysburg Address stands as the most enduring and powerful speech in American history. Lincoln defined the **purpose of America:**

> *...dedicated to the proposition*
> *that we are all created equal.*

In logic and philosophy, a proposition is a statement that can be tested—something that must be proven true or false. So when Lincoln said the nation was "dedicated to the proposition that all men are created equal," he was saying something brilliant. He wasn't just saying equality sounded good, he was saying it's a belief that must be **tested and proven** in how we live.

In other words: "We say everyone is equal, but are we living like it's true?" That's the real challenge Lincoln gave us: *To make our actions match our values.* And that's where character begins.

"The Gettysburg Address was shorter than my snack break."

Commander-in-Chef Quiz

Presidential Favorites & Tummy-Ticklers in 25 Questions

1. Which U.S. president was famously obsessed with jelly beans?
☐ Jimmy Carter
☐ Ronald Reagan
☐ Bill Clinton
☐ George H. W. Bush

2. What was Abraham Lincoln's favorite treat?
☐ Chicken pot pie
☐ Peach cobbler
☐ Gingerbread cookies
☐ Apple pie

3. Which president banned broccoli from Air Force One?
☐ Barack Obama
☐ Franklin D. Roosevelt
☐ Calvin Coolidge
☐ George H. W. Bush

4. Who was the first president to brew beer at the White House?
☐ Thomas Jefferson
☐ Andrew Jackson
☐ Barack Obama
☐ Ulysses S. Grant

5. Which president had such a soft spot for cottage cheese that he topped it with ketchup?
☐ Jimmy Carter
☐ Gerald Ford
☐ Richard Nixon
☐ Dwight Eisenhower

6. Which president reportedly had a sweet potato pie baked weekly?
☐ Bill Clinton
☐ Joe Biden
☐ Franklin D. Roosevelt
☐ George Washington

7. What food did Thomas Jefferson help popularize in America?
□ Mac and cheese
□ Fried chicken
□ Cornbread
□ Pancakes

8. Which president was known to eat fried squirrel in college?
□ Andrew Jackson
□ James Garfield
□ William Howard Taft
□ Jimmy Carter

9. Which president had a "midnight snack closet"?
□ Barack Obama
□ Joe Biden
□ Donald Trump
□ Bill Clinton

10. Which president enjoyed a dish called "corn dodgers"?
□ Zachary Taylor
□ Herbert Hoover
□ George Washington
□ Franklin Pierce

11. Who was famous for burning his toast so often staff kept backups ready?
□ Jimmy Carter
□ Joe Biden
□ Harry Truman
□ George W. Bush

12. Which president loved ham with redeye gravy multiple times per week?
□ Andrew Johnson
□ Bill Clinton
□ Lyndon B. Johnson
□ Woodrow Wilson

13. Which president reportedly drank a gallon of coffee a day?
☐ Teddy Roosevelt
☐ Calvin Coolidge
☐ Barack Obama
☐ John Adams

14. Who dipped sugar cookies in bourbon before eating them?
☐ Grover Cleveland
☐ John F. Kennedy
☐ Martin Van Buren
☐ Franklin D. Roosevelt

15. What was Franklin D. Roosevelt's favorite cocktail?
☐ Old Fashioned
☐ Daiquiri
☐ Manhattan
☐ Martini

16. Who had a peanut soup recipe served at the White House?
☐ William Taft
☐ George Washington
☐ Jimmy Carter
☐ Barack Obama

17. Which president was rumored to eat cornbread every day?
☐ Abraham Lincoln
☐ Millard Fillmore
☐ Andrew Jackson
☐ Zachary Taylor

18. Who had a backyard grill built on the White House lawn?
☐ Dwight D. Eisenhower
☐ Lyndon B. Johnson
☐ Bill Clinton
☐ George W. Bush

19. Which president loved fried peanut butter and banana sandwiches?
☐ Jimmy Carter
☐ Barack Obama
☐ George W. Bush
☐ None — that was Elvis

20. Who was known to toss M&Ms into his mouth during briefings?
☐ Gerald Ford
☐ Ronald Reagan
☐ Joe Biden
☐ Donald Trump

21. Who was pressured by the First Lady to eat salad daily, despite hating it?
☐ Jackie Kennedy
☐ Barbara Bush
☐ Michelle Obama
☐ Eleanor Roosevelt

22. Who said, "I never met a cookie I didn't like"?
☐ Ronald Reagan
☐ Barack Obama
☐ Bill Clinton
☐ Joe Biden

23. Which president was known for his cheeseburger obsession?
☐ Donald Trump
☐ Lyndon Johnson
☐ Richard Nixon
☐ George W. Bush

24. Who loved vanilla ice cream so much it was served nearly every meal?
☐ James Madison
☐ Grover Cleveland
☐ Thomas Jefferson
☐ Ulysses S. Grant

25. Who started the tradition of presidential M&Ms?
☐ Bill Clinton
☐ Joe Biden
☐ Ronald Reagan
☐ George H. W. Bush

Answer Key

1. Ronald Reagan

2. Gingerbread cookies

3. George H. W. Bush

4. Barack Obama

5. Richard Nixon

6. Bill Clinton

7. Mac and cheese

8. James Garfield

9. Bill Clinton

10. Zachary Taylor

11. Joe Biden

12. Lyndon B. Johnson

13. Teddy Roosevelt

14. Franklin D. Roosevelt

15. Martini

16. Jimmy Carter

17. Andrew Jackson

18. Lyndon B. Johnson

19. None – that was Elvis

20. Ronald Reagan

21. Barbara Bush

22. Bill Clinton

23. Donald Trump

24. Grover Cleveland

25. Ronald Reagan

Acknowledgments

Every book has its key influences, and *Bite Back Better* owes its success to two individuals—one in the kitchen and one with the pages of history.

My wife, Ann Marie, whose Italian heritage has blessed her with an uncanny talent in the kitchen, ensures every dish in this book is just right.

If the way to a man's heart is through his stomach, then Ann Marie took the express lane with no detours!

Over the years, her cooking has won me over time and time again, and she didn't just bring that magic to our home, she brought it to this book. She proofread every recipe, making sure they were practical, delicious, and worthy of a place at any table. To my delight, she also discovered that ChatGPT is surprisingly good at recipe creation, though she still gets full credit for keeping the culinary side of this book on track.

Bill O'Reilly, through his book *Confronting the Presidents*, provided the only historical reference I needed. As the most successful writer-historian in the world, O'Reilly delivers history in a way that is both accessible and unflinching, making his work the ideal foundation for this project. O'Reilly served as a reliable check on ChatGPT. I like to keep things simple, clear, and easy to access, and no other source was necessary.

To both Ann Marie and Bill O'Reilly—one who kept the recipes sharp and the other who kept the history honest—this book is better because of you.

PLH

Character-Based American Values

These are core values often taught in American homes, schools, and in moments of real-life learning.

- **Generosity** – Giving freely of time, help, or resources. Seen in everything from charity work to neighbors lending a hand.

- **Empathy** – Understanding and caring about others' feelings and experiences. Key to kindness, service, and unity.

- **Self-Reliance** – Believing in your ability to solve problems and take responsibility without always depending on others.

- **Kindness** – Doing good without being asked. Builds trust and brings people together.

- **Gratitude** – Appreciating what you have and recognizing the efforts of others.

- **Integrity** – Doing the right thing even when no one's watching. A moral backbone that earns lasting respect.

- **Perseverance** – Not giving up when things get hard. Rooted in the pioneer and immigrant spirit.

- **Respect** – Treating others with dignity, even when they're different from you.

- **Accountability** – Owning your actions—both the wins and the mistakes.

- **Compassion** – Not just feeling for others, but stepping in to help.

- **Service** – Putting others first, especially in families, communities, or through military or civic roles.

- **Humility** – Being confident without needing attention; knowing your worth without boasting.

- **Courage** – Facing fear, challenge, or pressure with strength and purpose—even when it's hard or unpopular.

These values are especially important for **teens and young adults** to explore—not just because they create better citizens, but because they build stronger, more meaningful lives.

About The Author

A popular TV guest, speaker, graphic designer, and videographer, Paul Lloyd Hemphill was born in Houlton, Maine back in the last century—yet he beat the odds—didn't disappear, didn't get canceled, and didn't end up as a field-trip footnote.

He graduated from college with honors in philosophy and theology, ideal training for asking deep questions, solving big problems, and occasionally baffling customer service reps.

Drafted into the U.S. Army during Vietnam, Paul received the Bronze Star Medal and the Vietnamese Cross of Gallantry, proof that integrity and grit aren't just talking points.

After returning home and stepping away from divinity school, he launched a decades-long career in marketing and media, where he wrote thousands of punchy radio and TV ads with clarity and punch. That same style drives his writing today— direct, memorable, and practical.

Paul has authored seven books, narrated four audiobooks, and co-wrote 6 books with ChatGPT.

He developed a national character-building video series for teens based on the most written-about event in American history, the Battle of Gettysburg, listed on his website as **America's 52 Stories.**

He's also the founder and chairman of American Education Defenders, Inc., a nonprofit dedicated to helping young people believe in themselves and their country while having the subtle effect of fostering a bond between parent and child.

He lives in Southborough, Massachusetts, with his wife, Ann Marie. They have two sons and three grandchildren who love to remind him that these appetizers are mouth-watering delicious, fun to share, and keep families together.

NOTES